HOW TO WRITE
HIGH STRUCTURE,
HIGH CONCEPT MOVIES

HOW TO WRITE HIGH STRUCTURE, HIGH CONCEPT MOVIES

*A step-by-step guide
to writing high concept,
structurally foolproof screenplays!*

Rob Tobin

Copyright © 2000 by Rob Tobin.

ISBN #:   Softcover   0-7388-2793-2

All rights reserved. No part of this book may be reproduced or transmitted in any form or by any means, electronic or mechanical, including photocopying, recording, or by any information storage and retrieval system, without permission in writing from the copyright owner.

This book was printed in the United States of America.

To order additional copies of this book, contact:
Xlibris Corporation
1-888-7-XLIBRIS
www.Xlibris.com
Orders@Xlibris.com

CONTENTS

FOREWORD 11

SECTION ONE
IN THE BEGINNING...

INTRODUCTION 15

CHAPTER ONE
    THE ABSOLUTE BASICS 19
CHAPTER TWO
    THE LOG LINE 26
CHAPTER THREE
    KNOWING YOUR STORY 32

SECTION TWO
STRUCTURE

CHAPTER FOUR
    STRUCTURAL BASICS 39
CHAPTER FIVE
    MORE DETAILS 47

SECTION THREE
BUILDING YOUR STORY

CHAPTER SIX
    YOUR LOG LINE 57

CHAPTER SEVEN
   THE OUTLINE/TREATMENT 66
CHAPTER EIGHT
   STORY ELEMENTS 69

SECTION FOUR
THE FIRST ACT

CHAPTER NINE
   BUILDING A SCREENPLAY FROM SCRATCH .. 77
CHAPTER TEN
   THE HERO'S BEGINNINGS 79
CHAPTER ELEVEN
   THE BEGINNING OF THE STORY 82
CHAPTER TWELVE
   THE OPPONENT 92
CHAPTER THIRTEEN
   THE HERO'S ALLY 94
CHAPTER FOURTEEN
   THE LIFECHANGING EVENT 97

SECTION FIVE
THE SECOND ACT

CHAPTER FIFTEEN
   TWO STORIES TO TELL 105
CHAPTER SIXTEEN
   REACTING TO THE LIFECHANGING
   EVENT 108
CHAPTER SEVENTEEN
   THE HERO AND ALLY 110
CHAPTER EIGHTEEN
   THE HERO STARTS GROWING 114
CHAPTER NINETEEN
   THE HERO TAKES ACTION 117

CHAPTER TWENTY
    THE OPPONENT STRIKES BACK 125
CHAPTER TWENTY-ONE
    THE HERO GETS A SECOND CHANCE 128

SECTION SIX
THE THIRD ACT

CHAPTER TWENTY-ONE
    THE BATTLE BEGINS BADLY 133
CHAPTER TWENTY-THREE
    THE HERO FIGHTS BACK 136
CHAPTER TWENTY-FOUR
    FINAL BATTLE 139
CHAPTER TWENTY FIVE
    EPILOG 144

SECTION SEVEN
THE NEXT STEP

CHAPTER TWENTY SIX
    CREATING A BLUEPRINT 147
CHAPTER TWENTY-SEVEN
    HIGH CONCEPT 154
CHAPTER TWENTY-EIGHT
    THE HIGH CONCEPT FORMULA 156
CHAPTER TWENTY-NINE
    "FIXING" LOW CONCEPT SCRIPTS 165
CHAPTER THIRTY
    IT'S A WRAP 173

To my family:
Marie, John, Brian and Josiah,
who have given me life's two most precious gifts:
love and a home,
and to Leslie:
wife, writing partner, resident stand-up comic
and love of my life.

FOREWORD

"Show it, don't say it."
—major tenet of good screenwriting

"If brevity be the soul of wit, then tonight we shall be very witty."
—Billy Crystal, MCing the Academy Awards

This book is exactly what the title implies: a step-by-step manual on how to write structurally sound, high-concept screenplays. It is a relatively short manual, because the point of this book is to get you writing as quickly as possible, by using the formulas that have been used to write nearly every successful movie in Hollywood history. In fact, I invite you to skip the introduction and go right to Chapter One, so that you can start learning and applying the tools of your trade *immediately*. In the meantime, in the spirit of Billy Crystal, let's get witty, and let's get down to business.

—Rob Tobin
Santa Monica, California
June, 2000

SECTION ONE
IN THE BEGINNING . . .

INTRODUCTION

"THE NEXT TIME SOMEONE CALLS YOUR WORK FORMULAIC... THANK THEM, AND TELL THEM TO BUY THIS BOOK."

The power of formulaic writing

"His writing was formulaic."
"The movie was so formulaic."
"Television has become so formulaic that there's nothing worth watching anymore."

"Formulaic" has become a pejorative term when applied to the arts and especially to the art of writing. But, let me ask you: if someone gave you the formula for turning lead into gold, would you take it, or would you self-righteously proclaim that gold created through the use of a formula is not worth having? For those of you who would shun the gold, I suggest you race back to your bookstore and get a refund on this book, because this book is specifically about learning and using the formula for creating all sorts of gold—both figurative and literal.

There *is* a screenwriting formula. Most commercially and critically successful screenplays use this formula in one form or another. If you want screenwriting success, both artistic and commercial, the first step is for you to become aware of that formula, to learn it backward and forward, and then to apply it with your own unique voice, style, personality, goals and philosophies.

Changing the Formula

Can you change the formula, fiddle with it, or disregard it altogether? Yes, yes and yes, though the results will vary greatly, depending on your level of writing skill. Masters of any art can flagrantly disregard the rules or even create new ones and still prosper based on their talent—Picasso, Stravinsky and Hemingway are three examples that come to mind. But for the rest of us, formulaic writing enhanced by our individual voices and personalities can be the key to our success.

This book will give you everything you need to know in terms of the elements that go into a well-written, structurally sound screenplay.

Lousy scripts can make money, despite the writing

Two final notes: as already mentioned, there are a lot of lousy scripts that get made into movies. Not only that, but some of these lousy movies do very well, sometimes even *extraordinarily* well, at the box office. The screenplay for "Titanic" is so weak that it was not even *nominated* for an Oscar, even though the film has made more than $2 billion worldwide and won 11 Oscars! But, for those writers who do not have a $250 million dollar budget, James Cameron attached to direct, and Leonardo DiCaprio attached to star, quality writing is the surest way to get someone to read and produce your writing.

Bad films aren't formulaic—and that's the problem!

Finally: most of the films and television shows people call "formulaic," actually *fail* to follow the formula outlined in this book. Such infamously weak screenplays as "Titanic," "Hudson Hawk," and "Ishtar" were tremendously weak in terms of the hero, opponent, hero's ally, character flaw, lifechanging event, second act character arc, subjective storyline and final battle scene—all elements described in this book as being part of the "formula" for writing success that I am about to introduce you to. So when someone calls a work "formulaic," you can respond: "No, because if it had been formulaic, it would have been a better movie."

CHAPTER ONE

THE ABSOLUTE BASICS

A SCREENPLAY CONSISTS OF SEVEN BASIC ELEMENTS.

These seven elements are:

- A hero
- The hero's character flaw
- Enabling circumstances
- An opponent
- The hero's ally
- The lifechanging event
- Jeopardy

Let's examine these in a little more detail:

A Hero

A person through whose eyes we see the story unfold. This is the person whose personal story forms the core of the screenplay, set against some larger background. Rocky Balboa is the hero of "Rocky." It is through his eyes that we see the story unfold. It is his personal story of overcoming his self-definition as a "loser" that takes place against the background of the world of boxing.

It is *always* the hero's story, played out against some larger backdrop. "Schindler's List" was Schindler's story, played out against the backdrop of the Holocaust. It was the hero's story that made "Schindler" different from "Sophie's Choice" which was different from *other* Holocaust movies. It is almost always the hero's story that makes one film different from another film in the same genre.

It's important to remember this, because you might be tempted to write a "Tornado story," and the problem with that is that there is nothing to distinguish it from other "bad weather" stories. The *hero's* story will distinguish one movie from another.

The hero's story distinguished "Rocky" from "Requiem for a Heavyweight," "The Boxer," "The Champ" and "Raging Bull." If you're going to write a "tornado story," make it, instead, the story of a fascinating character overcoming a compelling character flaw, set against the *backdrop* of a tornado.

THIS IS A CRUCIAL POINT. Developing your hero is the most important part of writing an interesting, compelling, commercially and critically viable screenplay. I'll go out on a limb and say that when you think of any film you've liked, you think of the hero: Bogey in "Casablanca," Tom Hanks in "Big," and "Forrest Gump," Arnold Schwarzenegger in "Terminator 2," Sally Field in "Steel Magnolias," Merryl Streep in "Postcards from the Edge" and "Sophie's Choice," Clint Eastwood in "In the Line of Fire." If you can't instantly remember who the hero was in a particular movie, I'll bet you didn't like the movie.

The hero's character flaw

The hero's flaw at the beginning of the story. This flaw hinders her in some way, even if sometimes the hero doesn't realize what the flaw is or *how* it is hindering her.

The hero's flaw is most often something which the hero views as a defense mechanism that she needs for her very survival. For example, Rocky Balboa defines himself as a loser because his father consistently told him he was ugly and stupid. This flaw, defining himself as a loser, keeps Rocky on the streets of Philadelphia, working for mobsters, hanging around other losers, without a romantic relationship, without a future, and without even an attempt to take advantage of his boxing potential.

This is definitely Rocky's flaw. However, from Rocky's point of view, it is the best way he has of coping with life. Realizing that he is a loser keeps him from making fatal mistakes. It keeps him from putting herself into situations he can't handle. That's why he doesn't train harder, because if he starts to succeed, it might put him in a situation where a loser like him could get hurt or laughed at or emotionally destroyed in some way.

So Rocky's flaw, believing he's a loser, protects him from getting hurt. He sees it as a realistic and safe assessment of who he is, and what he can do, an assessment that keeps him safe emotionally and physically.

Enabling circumstances

These are the circumstances the hero has created or found for herself, the circumstances that surround the hero at the beginning of the story and that allow her to maintain her flaw.

Again, Rocky Balboa stays on the streets of Philadelphia and in the worst boxing gyms, working for two-bit mobsters, fighting two-bit opponents, refusing help from coaches like Burgess Meredith, because this allows him to continue being a loser, and to avoid situations in which he might embarrass himself. It protects him from having unrealistic expectations or opportunities. It keeps him from doing things that a "loser" shouldn't even *try* to do.

In Rocky's mind, these enabling circumstances enable him to *survive*. And, since the hero's flaw does on some level negatively affect her, it is only by creating or entering enabling circumstances that she can hold onto that flaw.

An opponent

Someone who opposes the hero in getting or doing what she wants. In "Rocky," the heavyweight champ Apollo Creed was the opponent, because he opposed Rocky in getting what he wanted, which was to go the distance against him in the ring.

In "Forrest Gump," the opponent was the woman who Forrest was in love with, played by actress Robin Wright Penn. She was the opponent because she opposed Forrest's desire to be with her—she ran around the world trying to escape her own past and in the process escaped Forrest as well.

It's important to note that the opponent is not the same as the "bad guy." The opponent is sometimes even a "good guy." An example is "The Fugitive" in which Tommy Lee Jones played the opponent, and he was a cop doing his job.

In fact, the opponent is sometimes someone who has the hero's best interest at heart. An example is "When Harry Met Sally." Meg Ryan is the opponent because she opposes Billy Crystal's desire to keep friendship and love separate. It's when Billy Crystal realizes that Meg Ryan is right, that he is able to realize a much more worthwhile goal: being with Meg Ryan.

This is an important point. What the hero wants at the beginning of the movie is not always in her own best interest, and the person who opposes her in getting what she wants is sometimes acting in the hero's best interest. And these kinds of heroes are often much more interesting than the trite "black-hatted" and "black-hearted" villains of those corny old westerns and war movies.

Another very, very important point: the opponent is the person who instigates the lifechanging event that happens at the end of the first act. More about this later.

The hero's ally

The person who helps the hero overcome her flaw. This is the person who spends the most on-screen time with the hero. In "Lethal Weapon," Danny Glover was the hero's ally, and stayed by Mel Gibson's side throughout, helping him overcome his suicidal tendencies.

It's important to note here that seldom does the opponent spend a significant amount of time with the hero—rather, it is the hero's ally who has the most on-screen time with the hero. Again using "Lethal Weapon" as an example, Gary Busy was the villain, and spent much less time on-screen with Mel Gibson than did Danny Glover.

Another important element is the *method by which the hero's ally influences the hero*, or what I call the Ally's M.O. In "Rocky," for instance, Talia Shire was the hero's ally, and influenced Rocky by providing a positive role model—she changed her own life and thereby helped Rocky realize that change might be possible in his life too. Never does she actually *tell* Rocky to change.

In another story, the hero's ally might be a mentor or father-figure who actively gives the hero advice. In yet another story, the hero's ally might influence the hero by providing a *negative* role model: the hero's ally might have the same flaw as the hero, which allows the hero to see someone else undergoing the negative effects of such a flaw, which helps the hero to decide to overcome that flaw in herself.

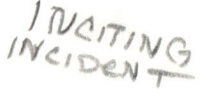
INCITING INCIDENT

The lifechanging event

An event at the end of act one, *usually instigated by the opponent,* which forces the hero to respond, to change his life in some way that's related to the hero's flaw. This lifechanging event always carries with it a challenge, threat or opportunity.

In "Rocky," the lifechanging event was Apollo Creed offering Rocky a chance at the world championship. Even though Rocky believed himself to be a loser, the magnitude of the opportunity was too great to refuse—even for him. He had to respond, and in the process of responding began to overcome his flaw, to redefine himself not as a loser, but as someone willing to "go the distance."

It is important to note, and will be reemphasized later, that the lifechanging event has to be a challenge that relates to the hero's character flaw. *The lifechanging event should force the hero to choose between her character flaw and the opportunity presented by the lifechanging event.*

This is one of the most important statements you'll read in this book, so let me repeat it: *The lifechanging event should force the hero to choose between her character flaw and the opportunity presented by the lifechanging event.*

A quick example: In "Leaving Las Vegas," although Nicholas Cage's character ends up dying, with never even an attempt at saving himself, there is still a point in the story, when he meets Elizabeth Shue, when he could have made a different choice. He could have chosen the opportunity of romance offered by Shue.

Instead, Cage's character chooses his character flaw, which is his suicidal determination to drink himself to death. A story in which the hero chooses her flaw instead of some opportunity, is called a "tragedy," as in Greek or Shakespearean Tragedy (e.g. "Oedipus Rex," "Romeo and Juliet," or "Macbeth.")

The relationship between the hero's character flaw and the lifechanging event forms the heart of any well-written screenplay. More about this later, but let me reemphasize, *the relationship between the hero's flaw and the lifechanging event is the most important element in any well-written story.*

Jeopardy

The hero has to have something to lose—either physically or emotionally. If there is no conflict, no jeopardy, no high stakes, there is no interest or excitement or tension in the story, and people will not be drawn into it. Things cannot come easily to your hero—she has to pay some great price to get what she wants, and the ultimate price is to give up her flaw, which she sees as a protection against the cruelty of life.

Asking a hero to give up her flaw should be like asking someone to take off their bullet-proof vest in the middle of a gun battle. Which is why, of course, the lifechanging event has to believably strong enough to force the hero to choose between her flaw and some opportunity, threat or challenge offered by the lifechanging event.

CHAPTER TWO

THE LOG LINE

What do I do with these elements?

You put them together into what is known in the industry as a LOG LINE. A log line is a one-sentence description of your story. Producers, writers and agents use log lines when pitching a story in Hollywood because nobody of any importance in Hollywood has time to hear a lengthy pitch, much less actually read a script, unless the log line is so compelling that they are willing to ask for a longer description of your story.

A log line is also what helps you determine whether your story is structurally sound. For example: "A meek and alienated little boy finds a stranded extraterrestrial and has find the courage to defy authorities to help the alien return to its home planet." "ET."

Please note, that not only does the aforementioned "ET" log line tell us what the story is about, it tells us what BOTH stories are about. Let me explain.

Objective and subjective storylines

The original title of this book was "Two Stories to Tell." That's because all well-written stories consist of two stories—the "objective storyline" and "subjective storyline."

The *objective* storyline is the backdrop against which the hero's story (the "subjective" story) takes place. In "ET," the objective story is about whether the boy gets the alien back to his ship. The *subjective* storyline is the hero's story, the story of the meek little boy finding the courage, conviction and self-worth he needs to be able to pull off the difficult and dangerous goal of saving ET, and of saving his own life in terms of being able to live it fully rather than always himself feeling alienated.

In "Rocky," the objective story is the story of Rocky training for and then fighting for the world heavyweight championship of the world against the opposition of the current Champ, Apollo Creed. The *subjective* storyline is the hero's story, the story of Rocky trying to overcome his image of being a loser. The subjective story, then, is the story of the hero becoming a better person, not better boxer or a better cop, or a better politician.

In "Lethal Weapon," the objective storyline is whether or not Mel Gibson's character can take down Gary Busy's bad-guy character. The subjective storyline is whether Gibson's character can find a reason to go on living.

In "Leaving Las Vegas," the objective storyline is whether Nicholas Cage's character will drink himself to death. The subjective storyline is whether Cage's character will find a reason to go on living—essentially the same as the "Lethal Weapon" subjective storyline, but the huge difference in the the hero's characters determines the huge difference in the two movies.

In "Hook," the objective storyline is whether the adult Peter Pan can rescue his children from Captain Hook. What's the subjective storyline?

STOP!

Pick 6 storylines

Right now, do this exercise—pick 6 movies and write down the objective and subjective storylines, just to ensure that you really understand the difference between objective and subjective storylines.

Stories that aren't stories and why

Okay, then, here's a story: a woman is sitting on a rock, looking out to sea. She's conflicted, feeling guilty about having abandoned her husband and children in order to pursue a career as a writer. As she sits on her rock, staring at the ocean, she works it out in her mind, and finally comes to a resolution of her conflict, deciding that she must pursue her dream and go on with her writing, even though it means that she must lose her family.

What's the objective storyline? What's the subjective storyline? There *is* no objective storyline, and this is important to recognize—that without an objective storyline, there is no external story for us to see. All we see is the woman looking out to sea, maybe with a frown on her face. This woman might be going through emotional conflict and anguish as great as that of soldiers in the middle of a war, but how do we know, and why should we care? What do we see on-screen that's visually interesting? Nothing.

Okay, a cop is chasing a bad guy, finally tracks him down, and defeats him. What's the objective storyline? A cop chases a bad guy. What's the subjective storyline? There *is* no subjective storyline. We can see spectacular special effects, gunfights, car crashes, bombs exploding, but there is no personal, subjective story or struggle. There is no one who draws us into the story, leads us through the story, no one to lend a personal feel to the movie.

The Eddie Murphy movie "Metro" fits this description—all car chases, explosions and gunfire, but no personal, subjective story. In fact the movie was so empty that half-way through they ran *out* of objective story, and even though Murphy's character had already caught the bad guy, the writers had to let the bad guy escape so that Murphy could to do the same chase thing all over again, because there was no subjective story to reinforce and deepen the objective story.

IMPORTANT: well-made stories contain *both* objective and subjective storylines.

The crucial thing to realize here is that only when Rocky (or any other hero) overcomes his character flaw, only when he triumphs on the *subjective* level, is he *able* to triumph on the *objective* level. He has to overcome his self-definition as a loser in order to apply himself sufficiently to win on the objective level, going the distance against the champ.

Is every screenplay written this way? Absolutely not. There are great screenplays that break many of these rules, and if you are one of those geniuses who can toss the rules aside and still write a masterpiece like "Forrest Gump," then go ahead. If, however, you are like the rest of us, it would do you well to at least be aware of standard screenplay structure so that, if nothing else, you know what "rules" you're breaking.

Recap: a log line consists of . . .

So let me repeat, because it *bears* repeating: a log line consists of the following: A *hero* with a *flaw* that keeps her from achieving a worthwhile goal, is forced to respond to a *lifechanging event* instigated by an *opponent,* and in the process of responding to that lifechanging event and with the help of an *ally,* the hero is forced to overcome her flaw, and only then is she ready to do one-on-one *battle* with the opponent to realize her goal.

One of the most important statements in this book

The hero's flaw has to be something that prevents the hero from responding successfully to the lifechanging event. Conversely, *the lifechanging event has to force the hero to choose between her flaw and the opportunity, challenge or threat presented by the lifechanging event.*

Examples of the hero's flaw from hit movies

Again, examples: Rocky Balboa is a loser who refuses to try to do better for himself, for fear of putting himself in a position that a loser like him can't handle. The lifechanging event, that of fighting for the world championship, is of such magnitude that even the "loser" Rocky can't refuse it.

BUT, Rocky cannot successfully respond to the opportunity unless he overcomes his image of himself as a loser. It is the overcoming of that flaw that allows him to respond to the lifechanging event by going the distance in the ring in the third act, one-on-one with the opponent. So, the lifechanging event forces him to choose between being a loser and the opportunity of fighting for the world championship.

Another example: In "Hook," the adult Peter Pan has forgotten who he is, which keeps him tied to the material world of overwork and neglect of his family. The lifechanging event is that Captain Hook kidnaps Peter's children.

The only way that Peter can respond successfully to the lifechanging event—the opportunity to rescue his children from Captain Hook—is to remember who he is and rediscover the imagination, faith and child-like joy in himself. He has to choose between his flaw, which is a type of self-induced amnesia, and the opportunity to rescue his children.

Examples of log lines

Okay, back to log lines: here are examples of log lines, to demonstrate how the best log lines usually include the aforementioned elements: *hero; flaw; lifechanging event; opponent; ally* and; *battle.*

A boxer (hero) with a loser mentality (*flaw*) is offered a chance by the world champ (opponent) to fight for the title (*lifechanging event*) but, with the help of his lover (ally) must learn to see himself as a winner before he can step into the ring (*battle*). "Rocky."

An overprotective (*flaw*) mother (*hero*) must overcome her own fears in order to allow her diabetic daughter (*opponent and ally*) to risk death to give birth (*lifechanging event*), then must fight to make sense of her daughter's losing battle against death (*battle*). "Steel Magnolias."

A jaded (flaw) WWII casino owner (hero) in Nazi-occupied Morocco sees his former lover (opponent) arrive (lifechanging event), accompanied by her husband (ally) whose heroism forces the hero to choose between his cynicism, his feeling for his ex-lover, and his once-strong feelings of patriotism (battle). "Casablanca."

STOP!

Practicing creating log lines

Take six of your favorite movies and create a log line for each of them, incorporating all of the aforementioned elements.

CHAPTER THREE

KNOWING YOUR STORY

STOP!!!!

Know the elements of *your* story

Don't read any further. Your job right *now* is to figure out as much as you can about the elements in your story. Take a pen and paper, or computer and keyboard, and start brainstorming about what the seven elements in *your* story are. You may not know all of them, but do your best to put as many of them down as possible.

And remember, *you can use one element to figure out what the other ones are.*

Using one element to figure out the others

Let me repeat: *you can use one element to figure out what the other elements are.* That means you can start with a hero, a lifechanging event, an opponent *or* a flaw, and figure out what the other, unknown, elements are.

For example: What is your hero's flaw? If you don't know what your hero's flaw is, ask yourself if you know what you want your character to be like at the *end* of the story. If you want your hero to be brave, chances are you want her to begin the story as a meek or even cowardly person. That, then, is your hero's flaw—meekness or cowardice. If you want your hero to be generous or compassionate at the end of the story, then you'll want her to begin the story as either stingy or coldhearted, as Bogey was in the original "Sabrina."

If you want your hero to be cynical at the beginning of the movie, chances are you want her to be patriotic, personally committed or enthusiastic in some way by the end of the movie, as in "Casablanca" where Bogey begins as the ultimate cynic and ends up become once more a patriot.

Who is your opponent? who is opposing your hero in realizing some deep-seated desire? If your hero wants to save the princess, then his opponent is going to be someone with a vested interest in keeping the princess for himself, or in having the princess marry someone else, as in "Ever After" or "Princess Bride."

If your hero is someone who wants to protect the President, as Clint Eastwood does in "Line of Fire," then chances are your opponent is someone who wants the President dead.

You can also figure out who your opponent is by asking who instigated the lifechanging event. For example, in "Hook," the lifechanging event is the opportunity for the adult Peter Pan to save his children, and that Challenge is instigated by Captain Hook, who kidnapped Peter's kids.

Screenwriting is, in essence, a process of asking and answering questions.

Now, answer these questions about your story:

WHO IS YOUR HERO?
Name:
Occupation:
Age:
Gender:
Where Born:
Physical Description:
Race:
Ethnicity:
Nationality:
Parents:
Pertinent personality traits:

WHAT IS YOUR HERO'S CHARACTER FLAW? What one flaw keeps your character from being who she can be, and accomplishing what she wants to accomplish? What flaw, what personality trait, fear, anger, hatred, prejudice, etc., has a negative impact on your hero, perhaps without her being fully aware of it? What flaw does she see as being not as a flaw at all, but rather as a viable way of dealing with life, based on her past, unpleasant experience of life?

WHAT ARE YOUR HERO'S ENABLING CIRCUMSTANCES? What are the circumstances, people, places and things around her that enable her to continue her character flaw? In "Hook," the demands of the adult Peter's corporate world allows him to keep his past identity forgotten. In "Postcards from the Edge," the movie business allows Merryl Streep's character to keep so busy that she is able to avoid confrontation with her mother and an examination of her own empty life and fears.

WHO IS THE HERO'S OPPONENT? What does your hero want at the beginning of the movie and who is *opposing* her in realizing that desire? Who instigates the lifechanging event? Remember, what your hero wants may not be in her best interests, and the opponent may actually have the hero's best interest at heart (as is common in many love stories such as "Sleepless in Seattle" and "When Harry Met Sally").

WHO IS THE HERO'S ALLY? The hero's ally is the person who shares most onscreen time with your hero, who will help the hero through the second act, and help her overcome her character flaw, either directly, or indirectly. In "Lethal Weapon," Danny Glover helps Mel Gibson overcome his suicidal tendencies.

WHAT IS THE ALLY'S M.O.? In "Lethal Weapon," Danny Glover influences Gibson by giving him a family to replace the family that Gibson lost. In other words, he gives Gibson a reason to live, by forcing him to live at least long enough to help save Glover's family from death.

In "Rocky," Talia Shire provides Rocky a positive role model, overcoming her own "loser" image and thus helping Rocky realize that it is possible for him to overcome his own negative self-image.

In "Steel Magnolias," Julia Roberts' willingness to risk death for the chance to have a baby, helps Sally Field's find meaning in her own role as mother and to face the dangers and sorrows of motherhood, such as losing your child. By the way, if you haven't seen "Steel Magnolias," do so. In my opinion, this is one of the best films ever made—it must be, because it's the only film I'm going to take time to recommend in this book.

WHAT IS THE LIFECHANGING EVENT? The event that forces your hero to respond, the one that is an OPPORTUNITY, CHALLENGE or THREAT that forces your hero to choose between her flaw and some opportunity presented by that lifechanging event.

JEOPARDY: What does the hero stand to lose?

DON'T GO ANY FURTHER UNTIL YOU'RE ABLE TO ANSWER THESE QUESTIONS!!! You may radically change the answers to these questions as you go on to other sections of this book and to the planning and writing of your own screenplay, but for now answer them to the best of your ability.

SECTION TWO
STRUCTURE

CHAPTER FOUR

STRUCTURAL BASICS

A SCREENPLAY HAS A BEGINNING, MIDDLE AND END, IN THE FORM OF THREE "ACTS."

The first act

The purpose of the first act of your screenplay is to describe and define the "hero" of the story.

Showing us the character flaw and redeeming qualities

First and foremost this means showing us the one, single, deep-seated character flaw that keeps your hero from being all that she can be, that negatively impacts her and perhaps even those around her. This flaw can be fear, bitterness, meekness, co-dependence, greed—anything that is serious enough to hinder your hero, and deep-seated enough to be very difficult for her to overcome. More about character flaw later.

In addition to the character flaw, you need to use the first act to show us your hero's redeeming qualities. These are qualities that mitigate her character flaw and make her either interesting and/or likable enough for us to spend 2 hours and 8 bucks watching her.

Introducing the opponent and hero's ally

In the first act you should also introduce your opponent and the hero's ally, the hero's ally being the person with whom your hero will spend most of her time, especially in the second act. The hero's ally is the person who will directly or indirectly help the hero overcome her character flaw. For example, in "Lethal Weapon," Mel Gibson is the hero, and Danny Glover is the hero's ally. Glover helps Gibson overcome his character flaw, which is Gibson's desire to commit suicide.

The lifechanging challenge

At the end of the first act, there is a *challenge* that is usually instigated by the opponent. This challenge is a threat, a challenge, and/or an opportunity. The challenge is such that the hero cannot respond to it successfully unless she overcomes her character flaw.

The hero will *try* to respond to the challenge without dropping her character flaw, but will eventually have to either abandon or overcome her character flaw it or else fail in her attempt to respond to the lifechanging event. The reason that the hero will try to maintain her character flaw is that she does not view it as a flaw, but as some kind of defense mechanism.

THIS IS AN IMPORTANT POINT, so let me repeat it: the reason your hero will try to maintain her character flaw is that she does not view it as a flaw, but as some kind of defense mechanism.

For example, let's say that a hero was, as a child, abused by a family member. Too young to *physically* escape, your young hero escapes *emotionally*, becoming withdrawn. Later, as an adult, your hero might still be withdrawn because this is how she has learned to deal with life and its vicissitudes. Even though we, the viewer, can see how this withdrawal is hurting the hero, the hero herself views it as a defense mechanism, and will not easily let go of it. The flaw is the way in which she deals with life—it's the way that she *survives* life. We'll come return to this point later.

The first act has traditionally been about 30 pages long, though of late there is a trend toward shorter scripts ("Titanic" notwithstanding), and the first act is now tending to be closer to 25 pages long. It has been suggested that the trend toward shorter scripts is meant to allow distributors to give an extra showing per day, especially of mediocre big-budget films that need to be shown as often as possible in as short a time as possible, before word-of-mouth kills them.

The second act

The 2nd act consists of the hero responding to the lifechanging event, with the help of the hero's ally. There are two stories to tell in this act: (a) the story of the hero trying to respond to the lifechanging event and to the opponent who instigated it, and; (b) the hero trying to overcome her character flaw with the help of the hero's ally.

Mid-second act confrontation

Halfway through the 2nd act, the hero and ally will have a confrontation that will determine the nature of their relationship for the rest of the screenplay. Remember, the hero does not regard her character flaw as a flaw at all, but rather as a necessary way of dealing with the world, based on the hero's painful experience of that world.

So, even in the face of a strong lifechanging event, the hero will battle to maintain her character flaw, and will battle against the ally's attempts to help her overcome that flaw. Rocky wants to fight for the world championship, but he's resisting the kind of change he needs to make in order to really have a chance of making a good showing.

This often leads to a somewhat antagonistic relationship between the hero and the hero's ally. The ally's job is to help the hero overcome her character flaw. The hero's job is to hold onto that character flaw while still trying to take advantage of whatever opportunity is offered by the lifechanging event. An example of this is "Lethal Weapon" in which the hero's ally, Danny Glover is at odds with Gibson because of Gibson's flaw—his desire to kill himself.

The conflict between the hero and ally escalates to a point about half-way through the second act (around page 60) at which time there is a confrontation and dislocation in their relationship. This confrontation can take many forms:

- the ally can threaten to withdraw her support unless the hero lets go of her character flaw
- the ally, with the same character flaw as the hero, acts out that character flaw so dramatically that it shakes the hero into realizing the danger of his own flaw
- the ally performs a particularly powerful act as a positive role model, which forces the hero to finally see the positive outcome she herself can have if she emulates the ally's behavior

The hero's choice

At this mid-second act confrontation, the hero has a choice. She can hold onto the character flaw and give up any chance of successfully responding to the lifechanging event. Or, the hero can finally open up to his ally.

In "Rocky," Talia Shire is the hero's ally. They do not have an antagonistic relationship. Talia does not ever directly try to change

Rocky. Instead, Talia acts as a role model. She rebels against her brother who calls her a loser. Rocky realizes that if Talia can change her self-image, then maybe he can change his. This middle-of-act-two confrontation forces Rocky to take stock, and to commit to overcoming his own flaw.

Following this mid-act confrontation, Rocky opens up to Talia. He says to her, "My father always told me I'd better be a good boxer because I was too stupid and ugly to do anything else." Rocky lets Talia, participate more fully in his life, and it's the most powerful moment in the subjective storyline.

From this point on, there is an acceleration toward the final battle with the opponent. The hero and ally are now working together. The hero is much closer to overcoming her flaw. And, though the opponent is still increasing the stakes and jeopardy, the hero is also getting stronger. Though by the end of the 2nd act we still can't be sure that the hero will win, we know that the hero now has at least a chance of winning or giving a good showing.

The point of no-return

There is sometimes one more important event before the end of the second act: the point of no-return. This is the point at which the hero is *tempted* to backslide. If the hero can overcome this final bout of self-doubt, she will be beyond the point of no-return and will head straight into battle with the opponent.

Note that the point of no-return is sometimes less of a temptation to backslide than a confirmation of the hero's having overcome her character flaw. The opportunity to backslide is presented, and the hero confirms her growth by refusing that opportunity.

The end of the 2nd act

By the end of the 2nd act, the hero will have finally overcome her character flaw, and will also have positioned herself so that she is able to confront the opponent for the final battle. The 2nd act is usually about 60 pages long. Again, however, a lot of scripts are coming in with the second act being shorter than that.

The 3rd act

THE 3RD ACT is usually 30 pages long, and consists of the hero, now unencumbered by her flaw, stepping into the ring alone, to battle one-on-one with the opponent. These battle scenes can vary greatly, from the physical slugfest of "Rocky," to the emotionally devastating warfare of the dinner scene in "Secrets and Lies."

This is all you need!
If you can use these simple concepts to write your script, then do so, without reading the rest of this book.

One of the best books on screenwriting is Vicki King's "How to Write a Movie in 21 Days," which basically uses nine "clothespins" on which to "hang" your screenplay. Ms. King then advises the screenwriter to then just write from one of these points to the next, stringing them together to write a script. I may not be doing Ms. King justice with this simplistic description of her marvelous book, but if you can do this kind of writing, then do so, writing from component to component.

I myself wrote a screenplay using Ms. King's wonderful little book and did a very nice first draft—I wrote the script merely to test her theories so that I'd know whether or not they'd be of use to me in my work with my own clients. I had to make several adjustments to the first draft (and in the process, developed many of the theories of my own screenwriting system), but Ms. King's theories helped me write a solid first draft, from which I and my writing partner wrote a final draft, and we are currently in active negotiations with a major production company on producing this script.

So, feel free to take just what you've read so far in this book, and write your screenplay—using these concepts, you will create a structurally sound screenplay and avoid the most common weaknesses of most screenplays.

To recap
So, to recap, these are the main points and steps in writing a structurally viable feature length screenplay:

Act One:

- INTRODUCE YOUR HERO.
- SHOW US HER CHARACTER FLAW AND HOW IT HOLDS HER BACK
- SHOW US HER MITIGATING GOOD (AND/OR INTERESTING) CHARACTERISTICS.
- DESCRIBE THE HERO'S ENABLING CIRCUMSTANCES.
- INTRODUCE THE OPPONENT
- INTRODUCE THE HERO'S ALLY
- INTRODUCE THE lifechanging event
- INTRODUCE THE HERO'S PERSONAL JEOPARDY
- HAVE THE HERO RESPOND TO THE lifechanging event
- HAVE THE OPPONENT OPPOSE THE HERO'S ATTEMPT TO RESPOND
- HAVE THE HERO'S ALLY TRY TO HELP HERO OVERCOME HER FLAW
- HAVE THE HERO AND HERO'S ALLY CONFRONT EACH OTHER HALFWAY THROUGH ACT 2, HERO FINALLY OPENING UP TO ALLY ABOUT THE REASON FOR HER FLAW

- HAVE THE HERO COMPLETELY OVERCOME HER FLAW BY THE END OF ACT 2
- HAVE THE HERO CONFRONT THE OPPONENT IN ACT 3, BATTLING TO THE FINISH

CHAPTER FIVE

MORE DETAILS

Second helpings

We're going to repeat some of the material we've already covered—think of it as second helpings. This is because by this point in the book, you may well be completely overwhelmed. It'll probably be valuable for you to step back a bit to reabsorb some of the concepts we've gone over. If, however, you feel that you've fully grasped the concepts presented so far in this book, feel free to skip this chapter. On the other hand, you may find something restated here in such a way as to make it clearer and therefore more useful to you.

Using one element to figure out the rest

As discussed earlier, you only really need to know one or two of the necessary story elements in order to figure out all the rest. And the process of finding out what the various elements are is a simple one. Again, it's the process that underlies all of screenwriting: asking and answering questions.

What is your hero's character flaw?

For instance, how do you know what your hero's character flaw is? Well, how do you want your hero to be by the *end* of the movie? Do you want her to be courageous? Then chances are that you'll want your hero to be meek or cowardly at the *beginning* of the movie. That means that her character flaw is cowardice or meekness. Overcoming (or succumbing to it if your story is a tragedy) is what the second act will consist of. Do you want her to be generous at the end of the movie? Then she might well begin the movie as a miser, and greed or miserliness will be her flaw. Do you want her to be honest by the end of the movie? Then dishonesty is her flaw at the beginning of the movie, and overcoming her dishonesty becomes the second act journey.

What is the lifechanging event?

Similarly, how do you know what the lifechanging event should be? What lifechanging event would force your hero to abandon her character flaw in order to be able to respond *successfully* to that lifechanging event? What lifechanging event would believably and entertainingly force your hero to choose between her flaw and some opportunity offered by the lifechanging event?

For instance, let's say that your hero's flaw is overeating (perhaps in order to fill an emotional hunger), and your hero weighs 800 lbs. Now remember, she has some vested interest in maintaining that flaw, (to her it's a defense mechanism that ensures her emotional and/or physical survival). What lifechanging event would force her to overcome such a deep-seated flaw? It would have to be a event that is impossible for the hero to resist. It would have to be so strong that she would be willing to take off her bulletproof vest in the middle of the gunfight that she calls life.

What if the hero's childhood sweetheart comes to town for the first time in years, and as soon as your hero sees him, she realizes that she is still madly in love with him? If the feelings of love are strong enough, the hero will respond to it, and the only way for her to respond successfully to the opportunity of being with that old lover, is to lose at least some of the excess weight that keeps her from being a viable romantic or sexual partner.

There is such a direct correlation in this example between the character flaw and the lifechanging event that it believably suggests what the second act is going to be about—the hero trying to lose weight (objective level), which forces her to deal with whatever issues made her overweight in the first place (subjective level), so that she can obtain her goal, which is to win the heart of the man (or woman, to be politically correct) she loves. Of course, you still have many elements to figure out, such as who the opponent is, the theme, the ally, and so on.

Similarly, let's say that you don't know what the hero's character flaw is, but you know the lifechanging event that is going to drive the script. For instance, let's say that the lifechanging even is the opportunity to play at Carnegie Hall. What character flaw would prevent our hero from taking advantage of this opportunity?

What if your hero is a drug addict who is too strung out to play well anymore? Now we know what the second act is going to consist of—her trying to overcome her addiction so that she can play and practice the way she knows she needs to. Remember, the lifechanging event is usually instigated by the opponent.

Thus, the chance for the hero to play at Carnegie Hall could have been created by an opponent who is trying to use it to destroy the hero, by forcing her to play Carnegie Hall while on drugs, thus ensuring her failure and humiliation. Or, the Carnegie Hall opportunity could have been created by an opponent who has the hero's best interest at heart, and who is hoping that the opportunity forces the hero to choose the opportunity instead of her flaw. In this scenario, the ally and opponent could be the same person.

Staying within the character's abilities

It must be *within the hero's power* to change her flaw. If she can't play Carnegie Hall because she lost her hands in an accident, then that's not a character flaw, it's a physical flaw, and there's not a hell of a lot she can do about it. It is foolish to equate her physical handicap with a personal flaw, and it is just as foolish to present her as somehow failing if she can't overcome that kind of handicap.

On the other hand, even in the case of the hero being physically handicapped, the real flaw might be that this physically handicapped former pianist has given up on *life*. There *is* something she can do about that: she can train a protege to play in her place, or write a piece of music that someone else can play. This way, even if she can't play at Carnegie Hall, her music can be played there (and perhaps she can help that other pianist with her career and/or personal issues).

Thus there is still a triumph to be achieved—or, possibly, a failure, if the hero decides against choosing the opportunity to write the music, and chooses instead to wallow in her own self-pity.

The relationship between the character flaw and lifechanging event

I'll be coming back to this point over and over again: This relationship between the character flaw and the lifechanging event is crucial—*THE LIFECHANGING EVENT MUST FORCE YOUR MAIN CHARACTER TO CHOOSE BETWEEN HER FLAW AND SOME OPPORTUNITY* presented by the lifechanging event.

Conversely, *YOUR MAIN CHARACTER'S FLAW MUST PREVENT HER FROM SUCCESSFULLY RESPONDING TO THE LIFECHANGING EVENT.* Otherwise, she can respond to the event without having to change.

This relationship between the hero's character flaw and the lifechanging event is perhaps the most important relationship in the script. This relationship exists in all well-made films, including dark tragedies such as "Leaving Las Vegas." In that movie, Nicholas Cage's character flaw is his suicidal tendency, as expressed in his decision to drink himself to death. The lifechanging event is that he meets Elizabeth Shue. Shue represents life, and Cage is forced to choose between his suicidal tendencies and the opportunity to go on living which is represented by Shue. Because it's a tragedy, Cage chooses his character flaw, and does indeed drink himself to death.

Again, I cannot stress this enough: the most important thing about screenwriting structure is the relationship between the hero's character flaw and the lifechanging event.

Who is the opponent?

Who is the opponent? The opponent is the one who believably and effectively opposes the hero in achieving her main goal, partly by instigating the lifechanging event. The opponent is not necessarily or even ideally a "bad guy," but rather someone standing between the hero and some important goal.

The difference between opponents and villains

THIS IS IMPORTANT: there is a difference between the terms "opponent" and "villain."

Opponents are unique, powerfully drawn, believable, intriguing, highly functional characters with their own believable motivations, flaws, and points of view.

Villains, on the other hand, are one-dimensional "bad guys" who most often exist in animated or live-action "cartoon" films such as "Superman," "101 Dalmations," and "Ace Ventura, Pet Detective," all of which were extremely successful and entertaining films, by the way, but none of which had any depth or drama to them.

You can choose to have a villain in your story instead of a fully-drawn opponent, especially if you're going to do a "cartoon" screenplay such as a broad farce or superhero action adventure. However, your chances of success will increase commensurate with the complexity and power of *all* your characters, especially your hero, hero's ally and your opponent. Even "Superman" would have been a more interesting movie with the use of an opponent rather than just a cardboard cut-out, "nasty" villain.

Different kinds of opponents

In "Forrest Gump," the opponent was the female lead played by Robin Wright. Not only is Robin Wright not a "bad guy," she is a wonderful, loving person who Forrest Gump dearly loves. She is also fully drawn, a young woman trying to escape a horrific past of physical abuse by her father. How can this sweet young woman be the opponent? Because Forrest Gump's main desire, perhaps even his *only* desire, is to be with Robin Wright.

She opposes Forrest's attempt to be with her, by continually running away—from her own past, but also, in doing so, from Forrest. Forrest ends up winning in the end, by simply loving her with all of his simple-minded being, so that she is forced to eventually realize that he is the right man for her.

The hero's desire

Another important point: the hero's goal or desire at the beginning of the script is not always a goal that would benefit the hero. For instance, a miser's desire might be to hold onto her money. The opponent might be a loving, generous person who wants the miser/hero to give her money to a worthwhile cause. If the hero's miserliness is causing her to be lonely, unhappy, mistrustful and unable to enjoy the wealth she does have, then the opponent is actually doing the hero a favor by trying to prevent her in achieving her desire, which is to continue being miserly at the cost of her own happiness.

When the hero's desire is actually negative or potentially harmful to the hero, then it is often the case that the opponent has the hero's best interests at heart. This kind of scenario often involves an ally who is also an opponent.

SECTION THREE
BUILDING YOUR STORY

CHAPTER SIX

YOUR LOG LINE

Log lines

Okay, so now what do you do with all these elements? Well for one thing, you can build a "log line," which is a term used in the entertainment industry for a one- or two-sentence description of your script. Log Lines are used not only to pitch a project to producers, execs or agents, but also to encapsulate the story in such a way so as to ensure that it is structurally sound. There's an old saying in Hollywood: if you can't describe your story in a sentence, there's something wrong with the story.

To create a valid log line, you need to include certain elements in that log line. Those elements include: Hero, Opponent, hero's ally, Character Flaw, lifechanging event and Implied Journey. For example:

> When an apathetic young man is framed for murder, he meets a compassionate woman who teaches him to care enough to not only clear his own name, but to try to stop the real killer, a terrorist with a nuclear bomb and a ticket to Disneyland.

This is the log line for one of my own screenplays, "The Server." I'll use "The Server" as an example later on, in the final chapter on "high concept."

Elements of a Log Line

Hero: young man
Character Flaw: apathy
Hero's ally: woman
Opponent: terrorist
Lifechanging event: being framed for murder, which forces him to care enough to at least try to clear his own name.
Implied Journey: the hero's journey to find the real murderer, and to learn the compassion he needs to be a better man.
Ally's MO: compassion.

It is usually important to include all the aforementioned elements to create a log line that will test the validity of your story. As a VP of development I saw many log lines that miss many of these elements, and these incomplete log lines didn't work. More importantly, if the log line doesn't work, then the script will not work. A hole in a one-line log line will be magnified by the number of lines in a script—hundreds upon hundreds of times.

One example that comes to mind is a log line that contained no people in it! It went something like: "Nature fights back against environmental abuse." This may seem like a ridiculous example, but often the extremes best illustrate problems that exist in the norm. The problem here being that the author left out at not one, but every important element, including people!

Identify the Elements in *Your* Log Line

Your job now is to identify all of the aforementioned elements in your story, and then to put them in the form of a log line. At this point, don't worry how long that log line is, even if it's a "log paragraph" or a "log page."

The point is to capture and convey the essence of your story, using the story's most important elements: hero, opponent, hero's flaw, hero's ally, lifechanging event, implied journey and ally's MO. Finally, edit the extended log line until it is a short, pithy description of your story.

If you continue to have problems creating a log line that really sizzles, be patient—the chapter on "high concept" will be of great help to you.

Creating a Log Line From Scratch

Can you create a log line from scratch merely by plugging in the aforementioned elements? Certainly. Let's do it right now.

- Hero: high school senior
- Character Flaw: insecure
- Hero's ally: dying father
- Opponent: domineering older brother
- lifechanging event: accepted to university
- Implied Journey: caring father helps the insecure young hero become confident enough to overcome his older brother's dominance and seek his own way in the world.
- Ally's MO: speaking from experience.

The log line? Something like: When an insecure high school senior from a small Canadian town is accepted by a prestigious university, he relies on his dying father's experience and wisdom to overcome his older brother's dominance and escape the gold mines that have trapped generations of his family and friends.

This is still a bit long, but the principles enunciated in the chapter on "high concept" will be useful in sharpening this log line. Does this sound too easy to be true? Admittedly, I'm an experienced writer and script doctor using my own tools, so of course it's going to be easy for me. However, it is possible for *anyone* to use this log line exercise to build the foundation of an entire story. The above log line was actually thrown together in a couple of minutes, specifically for this part of the book. Image how much better it could (and might!) get with a little work and thought.

Using One Element to Figure Out the Others in Your Log Line

Remember, also, that you don't have to know all the elements of your log line right away—you can know one or two, and then figure out the rest of them.

For instance, let's start out right here by picking only one element of a log line and go through the process of figuring out what the other elements can be to formulate an interesting log line. Let's pick the lifechanging event.

Okay, the lifechanging event in this instance is that (and remember, I'm making this up even as I write this) a young woman wins a huge lottery prize. Okay, now, let's start asking questions to figure out what the other elements are.

The first question: what opportunity does the lifechanging event offer? The chance to be wealthy. if our hero's already wealthy, the lottery really doesn't offer that much of an opportunity, so the full effect of the lottery will come if our hero is hurting for money, or at least not already wealthy. Or, perhaps our hero has rejected wealth for some reason—she may be a nun, for example, or her parents were wealthy and abusive, and she equates the wealth with the abuse, and thus rejects it.

Now, if our hero is poor, and the lottery solves that problem, the script is over by page 30: a poor young woman wins a lottery and lives happily ever after.

So, if our hero is poor, and the lottery would prevent her from being poor anymore, the flaw must be something that makes our hero *choose* to be poor. There must be a strong, believable, entertaining reason for our hero to choose poverty over wealthy. That way, the lottery is something that will force our hero to choose between poverty and the opportunity of being wealthy.

What flaw in our hero would make it undesirable, difficult or even impossible for her to take advantage of the opportunity presented by the lifechanging event? Maybe she's anti-materialistic. She might, as mentioned, be a nun, or other type of ascetic with a vow of poverty.

Or maybe she's from a rich family whose corruption has driven her to renounce wealth.

Or maybe she has so many friends in her lower-class lifestyle that she's afraid of losing them if she accepts the lottery money and the attendant inevitable change in lifestyle.

Or maybe her lover is poor but hardworking and proud, and she knows he would never accept being a "kept man" if she suddenly became wealthy.

Okay, we could go a number of ways here, so let me throw out just one of a possible myriad of storylines based on the only element we have to work with—the lifechanging event.

Maybe the lottery isn't an actual lottery, but rather an unexpected windfall that results from the hero's efforts. Let's say that our hero is a writer or other type of artist who finally "hits" it with a book, screenplay, song, whatever, and the windfall is huge, perhaps accompanied by fame and status.

If this woman has been striving for years to "make it," and she met and fell in love with her lover when neither of them were "making it," and now suddenly *she* alone has "made it," the stresses on *all* her relationships will explode into being.

If she is middle-class or even lower middle class, struggling with bills, enjoying the very unsophisticated pleasures of life, and enjoying them with other people of her social and economic class, then this windfall, the act one event, will cause an instant or at least very quick rift between the newly rich and famous hero and the still working-class people she loves.

Okay, we're getting there. Let's go a step further here and create at least two more elements: the character flaw and the opponent. Again, we have many choices, but let's arbitrarily go with the hero having a fear of rising above her present station.

Okay, who's the opponent here? The lover, I would guess. Why is he the opponent? Because he opposes the hero's desire to avoid success. Does he instigate the act one event? Sure, let's say that he submits one of her works of art (painting, song, novel, screenplay, whatever) to a publisher or producer, which is what leads to the page 30 event.

Who's the hero's ally? A neighbor and/or friend of the same economic class. Another woman struggling to cope with the harshness of their economically deprived life, someone who both understands the hero's fear, but who is also best suited to helping her overcome it, because she also understands the pain and frustration of being poor and afraid.

So now we have a hero, page 30 event, opponent, character flaw and hero's ally, just from knowing one element—the page 30 event. I could (and might!) go on to develop this story further, but I think that even as it is now, it serves as an excellent example of the way in which we can go from one element to a full log line in a very short period of time, just by making use of the relationships between the elements of storytelling structure.

Another important point here, however: don't be afraid to alter any element in the story if it makes it easier to write the best possible story. My changing the page 30 event from a lottery to an earned reward made this story work much more easily, so I did it. Whatever works, do it, and oftentimes it is not what you think it should be—go with the flow as long as you feel that it is helping you to create an interesting, powerful story.

Could we do a story with the lottery angle? Sure, though we may or may not have to force it. But, for the heck of it, let's do it now. Okay, our hero wins a lottery on page 30. The problem is, that if this is the lifechanging event, how can it be that it was arranged by the opponent? let's say that the hero comes from a wealthy family, a family who abuse that wealth, cheated others to get it and keep it, and the members of that family are so obsessed with wealth that they have ignored their own daughter—our hero.

So now we have two elements—the lottery win and a hero who is anti-materialistic because of her upbringing. We also have an opponent—either one of the parents will do, but let's say it's the father.

Wow we need the father to be the cause of the lottery win, which is precisely the element that is going to require us to force the issue a bit.

Let's say that the father is constantly trying to make his estranged daughter see the "light" and come back into the upper-class, materialistic fold. He visits his daughter just prior to the lifechanging event, to try to bring her back into that fold.

They argue, and the father, angry, throws a lottery ticket onto our hero's coffee table, saying: "Here, I bought this on the way over as a peace offering, but I guess it's too far gone for that now. Why don't you think of it as representing your life in this rat-hole of yours: all the odds stacked against you."

The father leaves, the daughter angrily balls up the lottery ticket and throws it into a corner. Then, days later, she discovers that the ticket is the winning ticket in a huge, multi-million dollar lottery. So now we have an opponent-caused lifechanging event that is going to force our anti-materialistic hero to choose between her principles (and bitter memories of her family's materialism) and, say, a $10 million jackpot.

Now, we're almost there, but we need at least one more thing: a character flaw. Let's say that our hero's flaw is her fear of becoming like her parents if she has their kind of money—falling prey to greed and cruelty and crass materialism. It is, more specifically, a lack of faith in her own good intentions that keeps her locked in poverty and failure as a way of avoiding the kind of temptations that her own parents fell prey to.

Now we've got a hero, a lifechanging event, a flaw, and an opponent—the father. How about an ally for our hero? Let's go with her lover from the last scenario—a good-hearted, hard-working man who can never seem to make it above middle-class or lower-middle-class despite his good intentions and good character. Suddenly his lover, our hero, is potentially a multi-multi-millionaire, and what does that do to their relationship?

Since he's the hero's ally and his job is to help the hero overcome her flaw, this earnest but unsuccessful young man has to be able to offer her something, have some way of influencing her. It could be as a positive role model, someone who is comfortable either with or without money because he knows who he really is, and he's centered enough to be able handle both situations without becoming either despondent or arrogant.

It could be as a negative role model—maybe he becomes so obsessed with the money that our hero becomes convinced that the money will destroy her life just as it has destroyed her parents' lives. Either way would make for an interesting story, depending on another question: how do you want your hero to be by the end of the story: rich and able to handle those riches, or; poor but able to appreciate what she does have, and not feel compelled to have her parents' kind of wealth and all of its dangers.

Again, the point is that by knowing a single element in your story, you can built on it, creating the other elements, then a log line, an outline or treatment, then finally the story itself, all based upon one single element, whether it's hero, flaw, lifechanging event, opponent, theme, hero's ally, ally's MO, whatever."

CHAPTER SEVEN

THE OUTLINE/TREATMENT

Creating a treatment or outline

The next step after the log line is to create an outline or a treatment of your story. An outline is exactly that—a rough outline of your script: the beginning, middle and end, plus the other major events in your story.

A treatment is more detailed—a brief description of every scene in your screenplay. Treatments can run as long as 20 or even 50 pages (I've been hired to write treatments at both these lengths). It's so detailed that you should be able to little more than add dialogue and have a screenplay.

Brainstorming

Perhaps the greatest tool for turning a log line into an outline or treatment is brainstorming, which is exactly what it sounds like—you sit down and give your brain free reign to come up with ideas, scenes, dialogue and any other facts about your story that you can think of.

You then organize those thoughts, ideas and scenes, chronologically so that they fit into your first, second and third acts in sequence. You can then expand those scenes, bits of dialogue and other facts as much as you can, linking them together, using one bit to help you decide what the next bit should be.

As with everything else about storytelling, the process is one of asking and answering questions. We know, for instance, that in our little lottery story, we would use the first act to describe a hero from a wealthy background. We know that our hero has rebelled against that background and is now living at a much lower economic level. We know that her lover is a good man but not a financially successful one. We know that the hero's father, the opponent, has abused his wealth, and ignored his daughter, and also wants to try to bring her back into his materialistic, greedy world.

Do you see how much we already know, just by knowing who the hero is, who the opponent and ally and flaw and lifechanging event is?

Start asking questions

Now, start asking questions. For example, what events and conversations would help us understand who our hero is? Think of ways that are both visual and entertaining, to show her fear of being like her parents, the nature of her relationship with her lover, her tortured past as a "poor little rich girl," and so on.

We can throw in the scene in which her father comes to visit her and leaves the lottery ticket.

We can throw in a scene in which she talks either on the phone or in person with her mother, to establish what the relationship between them is.

We can create a scene in which we see how much our hero genuinely loves her lover, and a scene in which we see how genuinely good-hearted but financially unlucky he is.

We can have a scene or several scenes showing our hero's friends, and how she and her lover enjoy their time with them, but on a very low budget since everyone she knows is poorly off financially.

We can have a scene in which someone is the driver of a luxury car "steals" the hero's parking space, and she goes off on him out of all proportion to the situation, angrily claiming that the other driver thinks that because he has money he can act any way that he wants to. This would help us see the beginnings of her anger toward her own rich parents.

Thinking up scenes

Just continue this process of thinking up scenes to show character, to show the lifechanging event, to show the effects of the lifechanging event and the struggle and drama and conflict it creates, the role of the opponent, the relationship between the hero and the hero's ally, and the method by which the hero's ally helps her begin to recognize and overcome her character flaw, the hero's past, the opponent's point of view, and so on.

Expand, ask questions, brainstorm, and soon enough you'll find that you have scene after scene, speech after speech, fact after fact, event after event, and soon enough you'll have a strong outline or even a full treatment.

CHAPTER EIGHT

STORY ELEMENTS

Don't read any further!

Okay, I sincerely believe that what you've read so far should be enough for you to write a structurally sound screenplay. In fact, I would prefer if you did not read any further, and that you go back to the beginning of this book and begin implementing all of the steps I've already described, writing down all of your elements, putting them into a log line, using that log line to expand into a short outline of your story, perhaps then into a treatment, and then finally into a screenplay.

More detail about *your* story elements

However, just in case you don't already have all you need to write the first draft of your screenplay, let's get even more detailed about what elements you'll need to have in your screenplay to make sure it's structurally sound.

The following is a complete, *extremely* detailed list of the elements that you can include in your screenplay. Leave out any element you want, put them into any order you like, as long as the result pleases you. Be aware, however, that what pleases you may or may not please an exec or agent to whom you submit your finished screenplay. But if you are genuinely pleased with whatever changes you make in the content or order of these elements, then that's the most important thing. Following this list of elements will be detailed explanations of each of them.

One note here about the importance of structure. I have two degrees in writing. When I was getting my undergraduate degree, I was in a program dominated by graduates of the University of Iowa's prestigious and very snooty writing program. The other people in the course wrote tortured, meaningful stories about people sitting on rocks, looking out to sea, examining their lives from the inside out. I wrote raunchy, "Fast Times At Ridgemont High" kind of pieces, including one entitled "S*M*U*T: Sister Mary's Undercover Tryst," about a horny nun.

All the other students hated me for what I wrote, and the professors resented me for my cavalier, non-literary style and content. But time after time the instructors would compliment me on my work because it was structurally bulletproof.

I had read books on structure and even when writing "S*M*U*T," the professor at one point commented that it was structurally perfect and read very quickly. The other students hated me even more after that, especially when they were forced to read my work out loud, each of them taking a different part. "S*M*U*T" was never as funny as when the part of the promiscuous Sister Mary had to be read by an uptight 2nd year writing student with aspirations of being the next Pearl Buck. (No letters on that, please—Pearl Buck is one of my favorite authors.)

Get your structure down right, and you're half way there. Make your story high concept (see Chapter Thirteen) as well as tightly structured, and you are ALL the way there. Even if your style is weak, even if you're inexperienced, if you have a strongly structured, high concept script, you can sell it. If you can't, e-mail me and I'll try to sell it for you!

HOW TO WRITE HIGH STRUCTURE, HIGH CONCEPT MOVIES

THE *ULTIMATE* LIST OF STORY ELEMENTS:

- POINT OF ORIGIN
- ORIGINAL CIRCUMSTANCE
- ORIGINAL CHALLENGE
- ORIGINAL DEFINING DECISION
- ORIGINAL SELF-DEFINITION
- PRIMARY EMOTIONAL STATE
- CHARACTER FLAW

IN ORDER:
BEGINNING OF STORY
1ST ACT:

- introduce hero (go against type, intrinsically interesting character, "hook")
- define hero's enabling circumstances
- portray hero's positive qualities ("dinner test")
- portray hero's flaw in several circumstances ("redeemability test")
- show how the hero's flaw hinders her and those around her
- show how deeply ingrained the OE is
- express the character flaw in several situations
- express hero's motivation and point of view
- introduce opponent
- introduce hero's ally if different from opponent
- introduce a life changing challenge that forces your hero to respond in a way that makes clear he is being hampered by her flaw.

2ND ACT

- delineate the storylines.
- hero's emotional reaction to the lifechanging event
- seeking out or accepting the help of a hero's ally

- hero's ally offers help, suggests or agrees to a course of action
- hero accepts or rejects course of action
- hero and hero's ally instigate first action against opponent
- hero balks, trying to maintain flaw and enabling circumstances
- opponent counterattacks, opponent's pov expressed
- hero's ally reacts to balk and opponent's counterattack
- hero's ally confronts hero over balk
- hero renews her determination to meet the challenge of the lifechanging event
- hero must convince hero's ally to give him a second chance
- hero gets second chance from hero's ally who's still mistrustful
- hero takes next step against opponent and against her own flaw
- hero's ally, mollified, bonds with hero,
- hero reveals some of her flaw to hero's ally
- hero's ally makes a demand of the hero on both objective and subjective level
- hero's ally reveals her own struggle, serves as role model
- hero and hero's ally take more steps against opponent who counters
- with each step hero overcomes more of her flaw
- opponent counters each of the hero and hero's ally's steps
- stakes, jeopardy and tension rises steadily on an objective level
- hero expands area of concern, opponent increases area of threat and strength of response
- the unraveling: hero falls farther behind, the low point of the objective story
- hero, out of desperation, breaks her own rules in an attempt to defeat the opponent.
- opponent or hero performs an act that cannot be responded to unless the hero completely abandons his flaw.

- hero must completely abandon her flaw or else perish—physically or emotionally
- second Circumstance
- second challenge
- second decision
- second self-definition
- new emotional state
- new behavior

3RD ACT:

- hero learns something about the opponent that gives her a chance at victory
- we the audience learn the full extent of the opponent's threat
- hero learns of opponent's true threat
- hero fully engages opponent
- opponent reaffirms point of view
- hero reaffirms pov
- opponent denigrates hero's point of view
- opponent points out hero's culpability
- hero admits to culpability, restates point of view
- one point of view emerges triumphant subjectively
- one character emerges triumphant objectively
- hero changes, faces future

SECTION FOUR
THE FIRST ACT

CHAPTER NINE

BUILDING A SCREENPLAY FROM SCRATCH

Seeing these elements probably doesn't do you much good—in fact, you probably feel rather overwhelmed. Good. You should occasionally feel overwhelmed—it means that you're taking risks, trying to learn and accomplish new things.

Elaborating on the elements

Now, let's elaborate on the elements in the list. And remember, you do not need to know *all* the elements in your story, because you can use the elements you *do* know to figure out what the other elements are, based on the *relationship between those elements*. In fact, let's illustrate that process in even more detail than we did in the previous chapter. We'll use the illustration of that process to define and explain the various elements on the previous list.

Let's build a story!

Let's begin with the *hero*, and actually build a story from that element, as a way of defining all the aforementioned story elements and to demonstrate how they work as they are actually applied, rather than just in theory. Now, be assured, the following story did not exist a moment ago, it is being built as I write this, just plugging in elements as I go along. Is this the best way to do things? Not necessarily. But, merely to illustrate the process, let me begin with the absolute minimum—one, single concept, and let's build an entire, detailed outline of a story, by creating the elements needed for such a story.

CHAPTER TEN

THE HERO'S BEGINNINGS

Our hero, the point of origin, the original circumstance and the original challenge

Okay, who's our hero? Let's begin with a guy who's going to war.

Our hero is a soldier, but not a professional soldier—he's been drafted. This is the point of origin for our story—a man being sent to war.

The original circumstance then becomes the war itself.

Now, during the war, the man is asked to risk his life to attack the enemy in some form—this is the original challenge.

The original defining decision and the original self-definition

The soldier now has a choice between fight or flight. The soldier decides to flee. This is the original defining decision.

The original defining definition is the decision by which the hero thereafter defines himself. This is the original self-definition that arises from the defining decision.

The primary emotional state

The soldier's definition of himself as a coward creates in him a primary emotional state. This could be *resentment* toward his government for putting him in a position that he did not feel he was capable of handling. It could be *fear* that someone will discover his cowardice. It could be *guilt* or *self-loathing*. Let's pick *fear*.

The character flaw

The hero's emotional state will express itself overtly—as a behavior of some sort. If the hero feels guilt, he may develop an exaggerated desire to please others, in an attempt to expiate his feelings of guilt. If the hero is bitter toward the government for having placed him in a situation he can't handle, he may act bitterly toward the world as a whole. If he's feeling guilty, then he may push people away, for fear of being found out to be a coward.

The hero may feel unworthy, as a coward, of having happiness or love or friendship. He may go into denial, and may lie, claiming to be a war hero, and perhaps build an entire life on this lie. There are many possible scenarios for our cowardly hero.

This is the overt expression of the primary emotional state—the character flaw. For our sample story, let's have our hero pushing people away, for fear that they will discover who he really is.

The beginning of the story

Now we have to choose the beginning of the story—whether to begin by showing the "backstory," or whether to do what famed writing coach John Truby calls a "running start."

Backstory vs. running start

Backstory consists of those events leading up to the beginning of the movie, which is the point in the hero's life at which we drop in. You can show the audience that backstory in just about any way you want to, depending on what's appropriate to your particular story. For example, let's look at "Forrest Gump" and "Rocky." "Forrest Gump" begins with Forrest as a child, and we actually watch him grow up to become the person he is for the rest of the movie.

In "Rocky" we begin with Rocky already exhibiting the flaw that holds him back, but we don't see how he got to this point in his life. In fact, the only reference to Rocky Balboa's past is his line half-way through the movie: "my father told me I'd better be a good boxer because I was too stupid and ugly to be anything else."

Most films use the second, "running start" approach, but it's up to you, because *you're* the writer, and it's *your* script. I myself prefer the approach of beginning the film with the hero already exhibiting the character flaw, because this way we hit the ground running, and have the joy of discovering who this person is and why he is the way he is. But, then, "Forrest Gump" is one of my favorite movies, so it can obviously work both ways.

For the purposes of this story we're creating right here, let's choose Truby's running start.

CHAPTER ELEVEN

THE BEGINNING OF THE STORY

The first act

Whatever your choice, we begin the movie with the first act. Note that an "act" is an invisible, arbitrary movie segment that never actually shows up in movies, unlike in stage plays where there is an actual intermission between acts. In film, it's just a way of looking at things, like: "There are two kinds of cars—gas guzzlers, and gas savers." In actual fact, there are *thousands* of kinds of cars, but dividing all those kinds into two categories might help someone in government to create environmental policy, for example.

Similarly, we use the term "three act structure" simply to understand and deal with script elements in an organized way. We could just as easily use a ten-act structure, which would be fine as long as it helps us create a viable story structure. Think of the three act structure as being the old "beginning, middle and end" that we always ascribe to stories even when we don't know a thing about structure.

Introducing our hero, the hero's circumstances and good qualities

The main purpose of the first act is to introduce the hero, her circumstances, and her good qualities. Let me stop here for a moment to discuss characterization.

Fully drawn characters

The traditional hero of old was the white-hatted (and white-skinned) guy with blindingly white teeth who was always nice to old ladies and polite to young ladies and protective of the town's citizens and with absolutely no apparent flaw in his character. He was fearless in the face of an army of bad guys, never tempted by the big-breasted, long-legged saloon girl, never at a loss of words and never did he ever have to go to the bathroom.

Good writers do not make their heroes "white hats" unless they're doing a farce like "Blazing Saddles." We need a flawed hero, because the story will be about a hero struggling to overcome that flaw in order to achieve a worthwhile goal against significant opposition. That may sound trite, but it forms the basis for just about every Oscar-winning film ever made.

Tobin's dinner test

However, we also need a hero who's either sympathetic enough or interesting enough for us to want to hear her story. I call this my "dinner test" because if I don't want to have dinner with the guy or gal, then why would I want to spend eight bucks to sit for two hours watching her in a darkened movie theater? I wouldn't.

Now, we can, of course, have an evil hero such as Tim Robbins' character in "The Player," because although Robbins' character isn't likable, he is *interesting*. And, remember also, that even the word "hero" is a bit misleading in that the main character of a movie is not always likable, strong or heroic—"Midnight Cowboy" and "The Player" are examples of films in which the main characters were quite anti-heroic.

The point is, though, that in order for us to want to follow the hero through a two-hour movie, she doesn't have to be likable, but she'd damned well better be interesting, interesting enough for us to care what happens to her and to want to have a two-hour dinner with her, listening to her life story.

An important note about introducing your hero's circumstances at the beginning of the movie: The circumstances have to be such that they allow the hero to continue her character flaw—otherwise our hero would have already been forced to change her character flaw, in which case the story is over before it starts.

Enabling circumstances

I call these circumstances the enabling circumstances, because they *enable* our hero to continue her flaw. However, these circumstances should also contain some seed of a threat, challenge or opportunity that will force your hero to eventually either overcome her character flaw or to somehow suffer significantly for *not* overcoming her character flaw.

If the hero fails to overcome her character flaw by the end of the story, the story is considered a "tragedy," such as Shakespearean and Greek tragedies or a movie like "Leaving Las Vegas" in which the hero is not redeemed and his character flaw not overcome.

So, we introduce our hero and his current, *enabling* circumstances. Let's make him an accountant. How safe can you get, right? Cowardice and courage are so far removed from such a career and such circumstances that it is completely believable that our hero would choose to wrap himself in the armor of such a safe life.

Now, something occurs to me while writing this that makes me want to go back and slightly alter something earlier in the storyline. What if our hero wasn't just a soldier who committed an act of cowardice, but was a Green Beret or a Navy Seal who committed an act of cowardice? This adds an interesting twist, because what we have now is a *physically dangerous* coward, almost a contradiction in terms.

Going against type

This goes against type nicely, which is something you should try to do as often as possible. If you have a hooker, have her be a stock broker or psychologist in the daytime. If you have a murderer, make him a priest. A philanthropist? Make her an ex-Nazi.

Intrinsically conflicting qualities

Always go for the built-in conflict, the intrinsically conflicting qualities in your hero, or a way to make her qualities intrinsically conflict with the circumstances. A perfect example is the novel and movie "Thorn Birds," in which a man falls in love with a woman—but not just any man, a Roman Catholic priest. The character's vows of chastity add an *automatic*, crucial and *intrinsic* conflict. An accountant falls in love, so what? A priest falls in love and the possibilities throw themselves at us.

A friend of mine recently (at the time of my writing this book) sold a script to Twentieth Century Fox. His premise illustrates extremely well this principle of intrinsic conflict. A radio psychologist who treats his call-in patients quite rudely, begins to take on their neuroses, just as he is scheduled to host his own national TV show.

This is a brilliant premise, and instantly begins to bring to mind someone like Steve Martin doing this physical comedy bit, adopting one neuroses after another—first stutter, then a tick, then a need to go to the bathroom every few minutes, various phobias, while the deadline for his taking over his new TV show approaches.

What my friend did was to ask himself: given that my hero is a psychologist, what one thing could happen that would most discomfit and endanger him while forcing him to look at his primary flaw? The answer is, of course, that the psychologist becomes himself neurotic, not only punishing him for being mean-spirited with his patients, but also forcing him to finally understand the horror of having these kinds of ticks, stutters, phobias, etc.

So, in our story here, let's create such an innate conflict by making our coward a physically dangerous, adept fighter/soldier. How? let's say that the point of origin may have involved our hero being a Green Beret, isolated in a battle zone with one of more of his allies. They've been under fire for hours, perhaps days, cut off from their own troops, dying one by one, and the stress is destroying even the toughest of the survivors. Then our hero snaps and commits some act of cowardice—perhaps flees instead of shooting an enemy, thus resulting in the needless death of one of his fellow soldiers.

Now we have a man who defines herself as a coward, and yet who also possesses the killing abilities of a Rambo. This is an Intrinsically conflicted and therefore intrinsically interesting character because what interests us is conflict—sports contests, war movies, the drama and conflict we create in our everyday life. A character who is intrinsically conflicted is also most likely intrinsically interesting.

AKA: "The Hook"

Another name for this is a "hook," which is any device which "spices" up a character or situation or scene by adding intrinsic conflict or intrinsic comedy.

"Peter Pan" is a nice little story, but how do you add a hook (no pun intended) to it to give it a fresh feel? How about a grown up Peter Pan who's forgotten who he is until his children are kidnapped by Captain Hook? This is the basis for Steven Spielberg's $100 million+ smash hit, "Hook."

How about the story of a man who is a mathematical genius? Boring. But, what if the mathematical genius is a moron in every other way, an idiot savant whose low-life brother wants to use him for his own selfish ends?

This, of course, is the Oscar-winning "Rain Man."

What about a mathematical genius who works as a janitor at MIT? This is the Oscar-winning "Good Will Hunting." A movie about a mathematical genius won't fly, unless there is some "hook" that creates a natural conflict in the mathematical genius.

"Hooks" can be applied to situations as well as characters. For instance, a soldier goes to war for his country. The hook? The warring countries have agreed that, instead of having an all-out war, they will place only two warriors on an island to battle it out, and whichever soldier emerges alive, that country "wins" the war.

Daren McGavin starred in a movie using this hook, and an additional hook was used—both countries sneak one additional soldier onto the island as an insurance policy, and McGavin ends up battling not only the opposing country's soldier and the opposing country's *extra* soldier, but his *own* country's additional soldier as well, because the additional soldier has to kill McGavin to prevent McGavin from revealing that his country cheated.

Using "hooks" is the way to make your piece "high concept," which means that you take an unusual, fresh approach to a subject, one you can describe in one sentence that captures the imagination and interest of a producer or studio executive who is too busy to read or listen to more than one sentence ideas. See the final chapter on "High Concept."

The hero's good qualities

Back to our story. We introduce our cowardly warrior, who is currently working as an accountant, and we see his good qualities in some little way—perhaps he goes out of his way to help someone pick something up, or he voluntarily takes the blame for the mistake of another employee.

The character flaw

Now you portray your hero's character flaw. Maybe the boss asks our hero to make the daily cash deposit, something usually done by some other employee. We see the hero carrying a large sum of money to a bank, with darkness falling. We see his fear.

Our frightened hero, holding the money bag as darkness falls, glances this way and that. He perspires and breathes heavily. Then he gets to the bank, and sure enough, he's jumped by a group of men who have been tailing him from work. But, instead of folding, the hero starts beating the hell out of the thugs! Why would we have him do this? Because he's a Green Beret! Yes, he's a coward, but he's also Rambo, and, when attacked, he acts on instinct.

So our hero takes out the guys in some realistic and yet still quite amazing way, maybe he gets slightly wounded which doesn't stop him or even slow him down. But, at the end of the fight, he's standing there, triumphant, but also still scared out of his wits, gasping, sweating, glancing around, paranoid, and he rushes to the night deposit box, shoves the day's deposits in and races back to his car. He locks the car doors and roars away in a panic. We understand that this guy is physically capable, but that something else is happening inside that makes him unreasonably afraid.

This is an intriguing way to introduce us to our hero, to his flaw, and it pulls us in. We want to stick around at least long enough to find out why this Rambo character is scared of his own shadow.

We've created an informative, fast-moving opening sequence just by following what might seem like a formulaic process of making sure we show the audience the steps in the storyline—hero, enabling circumstances, character flaw, and some hint of the point of origin in that we've shown this guy to be afraid, and yet also incredibly good at inflicting violence. We want to know more now—why would Rambo be a "scaredy cat?"

Of course, this scene needs more than just our hero beating up a bunch of muggers. He should respond initially to the confrontation with the muggers by trying to back down, maybe even trying to give the money to the muggers—anything to avoid a fight. But the muggers take the money and still persist in accosting him, maybe admitting that they intend to kill him anyway, just to eliminate him as a witness.

Even then, our fearful hero might submit, maybe even allow himself to be struck, and it is only when he realizes that his life is indeed in danger that he fights back. This way we see that his character flaw is indeed very deep-seated.

Showing how the hero's flaw hinders him

Now we want to show how the hero's character flaw hinders him and those around him, even in the midst of his enabling circumstances. So, we'll have to show him losing something because of his character flaw, but also being willing to take that loss, which is why he's still in these circumstances.

Maybe our hero's meekness makes him subservient to another character, or forces him to take unreasonable verbal abuse or neglect.

The last scene, the one at the bank, could be used to show several things—the hero's character flaw, how deep-seated it is, and how in a very real way it hinders him.

Show how deeply ingrained the flaw is

Also show how deeply ingrained the character flaw is, which it should be, since the hero has had time to let it *become* ingrained since the point of origin. Also, if the character flaw is not deeply ingrained, it's going to be a short, boring movie—the hero overcomes his character flaw in the first five minutes and we all go home after having paid $8.

Imagine our hero in his cubicle or office, and someone starts screaming at him about some mistake that wasn't even the hero's fault. The hero is humiliated—publicly, in front of other company employees. He has a chance to react, to fight back, especially since he is so physically strong and capable. Instead, he swallows his pride and takes the abuse, showing us how deeply ingrained his character flaw is. This will be especially obvious to us, because we will have already seen our hero's physical capabilities in beating up the muggers.

Show the flaw in more than one situation

Another point here—the character flaw should be shown in more than one situation and scene in that first act. This is because we don't want the audience to think that the character performs his character flaw only in a specific situation. We want to show that the flaw emerges not out of that situation but rather from the character himself. The flaw needs to be intrinsic, not dependent on outside circumstances.

For instance, if we see our hero become angry at work, how do we know if he is an intrinsically angry guy, or if he might, instead, have a lousy job or an abusive boss? But, if you show your hero angry at *work*, with his *family*, and then with his *friends*, then we can be pretty sure that he has an inner anger that is not dependent on the situation but rather on something in the hero's past.

Express the hero's motivation and POV

One of the most important things to do in the first act is, is to express the hero's motivation and point of view. A major part of the battle between the hero and opponent is the clash of their points of view, so we need to have *both* their points of view clearly expressed, either verbally or, even better, by their actions.

For instance, if you have a hero who believes strongly in doing his duty, and you have an opponent who believes that doing his duty has caused him nothing but harm, you are going to have a fundamental clash of points of view between these two characters.

Of course, you can also have both hero and opponent share the same motivation but have different points of view about how to express that motivation. For instance your hero might be a cop who fights for justice by upholding the law, and your opponent can be a terrorist who fights for justice by trying to destroy what he sees as a corrupt government.

What would be a believable motivation and point of view for either the hero or opponent? The hero seeks to atone for his cowardice in some way—perhaps by avoiding situations where he might once again perform a cowardly act and thereby hurt someone. There is also a touch of self-punishment, out of a feeling of guilt. So the hero's point of view is that he was wrong in what he did. He feels he deserves to pay for that wrong. Maybe he believes there is no way to atone for it, which is why he's hiding rather than trying to make up for his original act of cowardice.

CHAPTER TWELVE

THE OPPONENT

The opponent's POV and motivation

What is the *opponent's* point of view and motivation? His motivation is to "get his." What is his point of view? If the *hero* believes that he needs to atone for his past mistake, perhaps the opponent believes that he's been the victim of someone else's mistake or misbehavior. Maybe he feels that he's owed something by society, or the company, or *someone*, because of some past injustice done to him.

Now we have a hero feeling that he needs to atone for a past error, and an opponent willing to *commit* an error to make up for an error perpetrated against him. He feels he's owed. This conflict between their points of view can be brought out during the battle and during the second act.

A strong opponent should have a strong point of view, so let's make sure that the opponent's p.o.v. is rooted in some past event. What if he's been discriminated against because of age, gender or race? Maybe he feels that his only recourse against such discrimination is to be as dishonest as the people who discriminated against him. This could be reinforced by the fact that he sees many examples of dishonest people succeeding wildly, apparently because of their dishonesty.

Introduce the opponent

So we introduce the opponent. At the same time, we can use the opponent to introduce the seed of danger that is contained within the enabling circumstance. How? By introducing an opponent and the threat that that opponent poses to our hero and to our hero's enabling circumstances. We use that threat to show how the hero's character flaw is hindering him, because we see him unable or at least unwilling to respond to that threat.

So, let's introduce the opponent by showing him threatening or abusing the hero in some way—not necessarily physically, but perhaps emotionally. Maybe the opponent is making fun of the hero, suckering him into doing favors for him, holding him up to ridicule, getting the hero in trouble or using him as an alibi or patsy. Perhaps the opponent simply makes an unreasonable or unfair demand that the hero is too afraid to refuse.

This demand can be as simple as the opponent asking the hero to make an accounting entry that seems a little iffy—claiming something as a refundable business expense when in fact it's a personal expense. This can set the tone for the hero's cowardice, the opponent's control over the hero, and the opponent's general demeanor and opposing point of view. We can even tie this in later by having the hero's entry of these questionable expenses be part of the evidence that damns the opponent, or perhaps even, in the short run, seems to implicate the hero.

CHAPTER THIRTEEN

THE HERO'S ALLY

Introduce the hero's ally

*I*ntroduce the hero's ally if different from the opponent. In some stories, such as love stories, the opponent and the hero's ally are the same character. An example is "When Harry Met Sally" where Meg Ryan both opposes Billy Crystal's desire to keep friendship and love separate, and also helps him overcome his character flaw by refusing to buy into his ridiculous claim that falling in love ruins friendship.

The hero's ally is that third character who serves as a catalyst, sounding board, mentor, role model and/or touchstone for the hero. This is usually the character with whom the hero spends the most time onscreen, especially during the second act, so this is an extremely important character.

It should be noted, as well, that the choice of hero's ally is important in the process of casting and "packaging" a movie. "Packaging" means attaching name stars and/or director to a script before going in to pitch the script to producers or execs. If you create an interesting hero and hero's ally, making them challenging and interesting roles with an interesting and challenging relationship between them, you'll have a better chance of attracting actors who can help you sell the movie.

Challenging roles attract good actors

Don't make any character in your story *impossible* to portray, but give each major character the kind of scenes that, if acted well, will make the role challenging, and bring acclaim for managing such a challenging role. Actors often tell their agents to look for "Oscar" roles for them—roles that will stretch them enough so that critics will be impressed. Think of "Forrest Gump," "Silence of the Lambs," "Gandhi" and "Charlie," all difficult roles that earned the actors Oscars.

In a more commercial vein, "Lethal Weapon" "48 Hours," "Beverly Hills Cop" and "Die Hard" are good examples of movies in which the hero spends most of his time with the ally rather than with the opponent. *In fact in most well-written movies, the opponent spends far less time on screen than does the hero's ally.*

It's clear, then, that the hero's ally is a critically important character, without whom the hero cannot learn how to overcome the flaw that keeps him from being able to successfully battle the opponent. The ally's job is to *prepare* the hero for the battle, by helping the hero strip away the flaw that's holding the hero back.

In "Rocky," Talia Shire's character didn't get into the ring to help Rocky fight his opponent Apollo Creed. But, by her positive example, she helps Rocky overcome his loser's attitude before he gets into the ring.

In the final scenes of "Lethal Weapon," Mel Gibson faces off one-on-one against Gary Busy, but it is Danny Glover who helps him overcome the death wish that would have prevented Gibson from living long enough to battle Busy.

The ally must lead the hero through a purifying fire that cleanses the hero of his weaknesses, allowing him to enter the ring against his opponent without encumbrances, distractions, weaknesses, fears, etc.

For our example, let's pick, as our hero's ally, the president of the company our hero works for. The reasons for this will become obvious as we get to the second act.

CHAPTER FOURTEEN

THE LIFECHANGING EVENT

Introduce the lifechanging event

Introduce the lifechanging event. *This is one of the most important elements in your story,* and is the culmination of the first act. The lifechanging event can be a challenge, a threat or an opportunity, and *it must prevent the hero from continuing his current life as he knows it.* This is a crucial point here, so let's repeat it—*the lifechanging event at the end of the first act should prevent the hero from continuing his life as he knows it.*

Unless you manage this element well, you will not have a strong second act, and therefore you will not have a strong third act. I cannot overemphasize the importance of a strong lifechanging event. It *must* force your hero to change his life in some way. It *must* force your hero to choose between his character flaw and some opportunity offered by the lifechanging event.

Even if your hero chooses his flaw instead of the opportunity, it should still change his life. In, for instance, "Leaving Las Vegas," the hero was already determined to kill himself before he experiences the lifechanging event in the form of meeting Elizabeth Shue's character.

However, meeting Shue forced the hero to even more fully commit to his suicide, because now he actually had something to live for, and STILL decides to kill himself. This is an important change. Before meeting Shue, Cage was a man choosing to kill himself because he had nothing to live for. After meeting Shue, Cage chooses to kill himself despite having something very definite to life for.

The job of the lifechanging event is to magnify the consequences of the hero's character flaw to the point at which the negative consequences outweigh whatever benefit the hero derives from the character flaw.

This is crucial, so I suggest you reread the last sentence.

In "Rocky," the consequence of Rocky Balboa's loser mentality was confined to his own life. Very few people cared about those consequences or were affected by them. The lifechanging challenge, in the form of the opportunity to fight for the world championship, magnified the consequences a thousand fold.

If Rocky continues to be irresponsible after the lifechanging event, he will shame himself in front of the entire country, the entire *world*, and miss what may be the greatest opportunity that will ever come his way. The consequences of his flaw have been magnified past the point at which Rocky is willing to endure them any longer.

In "Leaving Las Vegas," of course, the story being a tragedy, the hero still chooses his character flaw, even when the lifechanging event has magnified the consequences of it: after meeting Elizabeth Shue, Cage now stands to lose not just his own rather empty life, but now stands to lose the chance to be with Shue.

In "Rocky," Rocky Balboa always had the opportunity to change, to train hard and do well in boxing. But that opportunity was never strong enough to prompt him to try to overcome his flaw. Then came the lifechanging event: the opportunity to fight for the championship of the world. Failing to accept that opportunity means being shamed in front of the entire world. The consequences of not reacting to the lifechanging event become stronger than the consequences of giving up his flaw.

Again, *the job of the lifechanging event is to magnify the consequences of the hero's character flaw to the point at which the negative consequences outweigh whatever benefit the hero derives from the character flaw.*

It is important that this lifechanging event be relevant to the rest of the elements in the story. For instance, if the lifechanging event is that the hero has to disarm a nuclear bomb, and the hero's flaw is that he overeats, then there is no obvious relationship or conflict between those two elements. If, however, the hero's flaw is cowardice, then there is an immediate and obvious conflict between disarming a nuclear bomb and the hero being a coward.

On the other hand, if the hero's flaw is overeating, then the lifechanging event should be something like running into an old flame and realizing that weighing 600 lbs. is going to get into the way of winning his old flame back. Thus the hero has the incentive to try to overcome his flaw because now the consequences of it have been magnified, and he's being forced to choose between his flaw and some opportunity offered by the lifechanging event.

THIS IS ANOTHER CRUCIAL POINT. The character's flaw must relate to the lifechanging event. The flaw must be such that it prevents your hero from responding to the lifechanging event successfully. If a 600 pound man who overeats in order to satisfy some emotional need, faces the lifechanging event of having to write a bestselling novel, you've got a big problem: the hero can write the book without missing a bite. He can respond to the lifechanging event, and still maintain his character flaw.

Again, the three most important elements in your story are going to be your hero, your hero's character flaw, and the lifechanging event at the end of act one. Even more important is the relationship between these elements. And, again, the relationship has to be that the hero's flaw negatively affects him, is deep-seated, and prevents him from responding to the lifechanging event. Alternatively, the lifechanging event has to be one that forces your main character to either overcome her character flaw or, as in a tragedy, to succumb completely to it.

The lifechanging event must be something that your hero cannot just walk away from. If your hero is a coward, and he discovers that a nuclear bomb has been planted nearby, he could well ignore the bomb and flee. In fact, if cowardice is his flaw, it seems *natural* that he would flee. This is obviously not a particularly good lifechanging event, because instead of forcing your hero to change his life, it merely reinforces the hero's flaw.

So you need an additional element that forces your cowardly hero to respond. Perhaps his family is endangered by the bomb, or perhaps he himself is endangered by it, unable to flee, and he's therefore forced to respond with heroism if he expects to be able to live through the ordeal. And, of course, there has to be some possibility of her being *able* to defuse the bomb. Otherwise, trying to defuse the bomb amounts to suicide. That means that he has to have some experience which would enable him, above all others, to defuse the bomb or force someone else to defuse it.

Your hero must be *able* to respond to the lifechanging event

This is another important point that bears repeating: your hero must have the *ability* to respond to the lifechanging event. If your hero is a coward, don't have his lifechanging event be that he has to single-handedly defeat the Red Chinese Army. Yes, to do so would certainly be a sign that he's overcome his cowardice, but since it's not possible for anyone on Earth to do so, it becomes an *invalid lifechanging event* because it's impossible for him to successfully meet the challenge.

So, let's pick a lifechanging event for our cowardly Green Beret/accountant. Since the hero's enabling circumstances are the accounting office of a mid-level company, then let's make it there that the lifechanging event takes place. That way, his enabling circumstances will be directly threatened, which is part of what will motivate the hero to respond to the lifechanging event.

Let's say that the opponent financially ransacks the company for which the hero and opponent work The opponent steals millions of dollars in pension fund money and other funds without which the company will go broke. The employees now stand to lose their jobs and their life savings, which are tied up in the company's pension and 401k funds. This is a definite and believable lifechanging event to the hero, to his enabling circumstance and to his character flaw. It's a good lifechanging event because it's going to force him to choose between his cowardice and the threat presented by the lifechanging event, the threat of losing his enabling circumstances.

Now, the lifechanging event kicks the story into the second act, and also energizes the story in terms of jeopardy, tension, drama and conflict. Up to this point we've basically seen the hero, the hero's circumstances, the hero's flaw and mitigating good qualities, the opponent and theme defined, and we've seen how the hero has created a set of enabling circumstances in which he can safely operate with his flaw intact. The lifechanging event threatens the hero's enabling circumstances.

We're done with the first act, but let me recap once more before we go on to the second act. In the first act, we should:

- be introduced to the hero and to the one character flaw that drives him and the story, the resolution of this flaw being what the real story is about.

- see the hero's flaw expressed in at least three very different circumstances in order to be sure that the flaw is in him, and not simply the result of a specific circumstance such as a lousy job, rough day or bad relationship.

- see some mitigating good and/or interesting qualities in the hero. They should be qualities that make him interesting and/or likable enough for us to want to spend two hours to find out what is going to happen to him.

- clearly see the hero's enabling circumstances and HOW those circumstances enable him to preserve and express his flaw.

- be introduced to the opponent by at least the end of the first act, and we should see that it is the opponent who instigates the lifechanging event.

- be introduced to the dynamic character either in the first act or very soon after the lifechanging event, early in the second act.

- see the lifechanging event at the end of the first act, instigated by the opponent. The lifechanging event should force the hero to respond, and to respond in such a way that he has to overcome his flaw in order to respond to the lifechanging event *successfully*. The question to ask is: will the hero's flaw prevent him from successfully responding to the lifechanging event? If the answer is "no," then you have to change the lifechanging event and/or the character flaw.

SECTION FIVE
THE SECOND ACT

CHAPTER FIFTEEN

TWO STORIES TO TELL

Delineate the storylines: objective vs. subjective storylines

The first thing we need to do in the 2nd act is to delineate the storylines. Let me explain this concept.

In any well-written story, there are two storylines, the "objective" and "subjective." *Creating two viable, intertwining, mutually supporting storylines is one of the most important elements of storytelling.*

The Objective Storyline is the story of the hero's physical struggle to respond to the lifechanging event. In "Rocky," the objective storyline is Rocky Balboa's physical preparation for the boxing match.

The *Subjective* Storyline is the hero's struggle to overcome his character flaw. In "Rocky," the subjective storyline is Rocky's struggle to overcome his self-image as a loser.

NOTE: the solution to the hero's flaw shouldn't exist on the *objective* level. Burgess Meredith trains Rocky on the *objective* level—how to move, how to punch, how to block, how to build up his endurance. So why isn't that enough? Because Rocky's flaw isn't that he's a lousy boxer. His flaw is *personal*, which means that it's *subjective*. A hero's flaw should always be subjective, personal. If a hero's flaw can be fixed merely by rearranging some things in the outside world, or on the purely physical level, it's the wrong flaw.

Look at it this way: every boxing movie is going to be about a boxer trying to be a better boxer, trying to win on the physical level. What differentiates one boxing movie from another, or one way movie from another, or one love story from another, is the hero's personal flaw and the journey that the hero has to undertake to overcome that flaw.

The subjective level is the level on which the hero works out his problems. The objective level is the level on which the hero demonstrates that he's overcome his flaw. The *objective* level is the level on which the hero gets to demonstrate what he's learned on the *subjective* level.

NOTE: while the resolution lies on the subjective level, the commercially viable "hook" of a movie almost always lies on the *objective* level. Let me repeat that: a movie's "hook" almost always lies on the objective level.

The chance for a title shot ("Rocky"), the chance to confront the secrets and lies of a family in denial ("Secrets and Lies"), a daughter's death ("Steel Magnolias")—all of these exist in the objective, external world. Without such an objective storyline, you might just as well have a hero sitting alone on a rock, peering out to sea, experiencing great inner conflict, with all of the attendant lack of excitement and involvement for the viewing audience.

In "Thorn Birds," the priest's flaw is that he is having a conflict of faith. But it is only when that conflict expresses itself in the real world, in the form of an affair, that the story really takes off. The priest having the affair is the hook.

One more important point about the subjective storyline: it is almost always, on some level, the search for love. Rocky wants to be called a winner instead of a loser, which is a blatant call for love. Our soldier hero wants to be forgiven for the death of his men—in other words he wants to be loved despite his youthful mistake.

However, it is only when that struggle for love emerges on the *objective* level that the story really starts. Rocky merely dating Adrienne is not enough to make a movie. Rocky fighting for the world championship of the world as a way of proving that he isn't a loser and that he deserves happiness and respect and love—*that* is a story.

CHAPTER SIXTEEN

REACTING TO THE LIFECHANGING EVENT

The ticking clock

The objective storyline also often provides the ticking clock. Rocky has to overcome his flaw *by fight time*, or else he's going to be dead meat in the ring. Although many people sneer at the "ticking clock" device (the deadline that the hero has to meet), it is a powerful tool if used right. After all, all stories take place in space and time, so why not make sure the place and time are used to their best advantage?

The hero's emotional reaction to the lifechanging event

Back to our story: the first event in the second act is the hero's emotional reaction to the lifechanging event—denial, anger, fear, despair, amusement, arrogance, fatalism, whatever.

The hero's physical reaction to the lifechanging event: seeking out the ally

The opponent's already taken his first step, by instigating the lifechanging event that immediately puts the hero and opponent into opposition. So, after his *emotional* reaction, the hero must *physically* react to the opponent's instigation of the lifechanging challenge. That response is usually to *seek out the hero's ally* to help him meet the lifechanging event. More exactly, the hero seeks out an ally or turns to an ally who is already present, in the hope of finding a way to either avoid the lifechanging challenge, or to meet it without giving up his character flaw.

Let me repeat that: initially the hero seeks out the ally as a desperate attempt to meet the lifechanging challenge without having to actually give up his character flaw. The irony is that the hero is unconsciously seeking out the one person *best suited* to help the hero overcome that same, exact flaw.

CHAPTER SEVENTEEN

THE HERO AND ALLY

The ally's job

The hero's ally's job is to help the hero get rid of what the hero wants most to keep: his character flaw. Thus we already have a built-in conflict. And, by the way, this is usually the most interesting conflict in the story.

Who cares if Rocky wins the fight or not? Obviously, since he didn't win the fight, and we still loved the movie, his winning the fight wasn't that important. It was Rocky's victory over his own flaw that made the movie worthwhile, that made Rocky's battle a victory despite losing in the ring.

If the lifechanging challenge is a good one, it will force the hero will react to it. But the hero will always be on the verge of drawing back if he sees a threat to his character flaw and/or to his enabling circumstances.

Ally suggests a course of action

Once the hero has sought out the ally for help, the ally will assume that the hero actually *wants* help. Thus the ally will *suggest a course of action*. OR:, as in Rocky, the ally will *indirectly* and perhaps even *inadvertently* suggest a course of action *by virtue of their behavior*.

For example, it is Adrienne changing her own life that inspires in Rocky an idea of how to handle his own flaw—by changing in the same way that Adrienne does, namely by abandoning the concept of being a loser. Again, every hero's ally has an MO, a way of operating, a way of influencing the hero—by example, by instruction, by negative example, by intimidation, whatever.

Hero accepts or rejects course of action and Hero balks

The hero will either accept or reject the course of action. The hero will accept the course of action if he fails to recognize that it threatens his character flaw and his enabling circumstances.

The hero will balk as soon as he recognize a threat to his character flaw and/or enabling circumstances. If he balks immediately, then the hero's ally might carry out the course of action by herself, and in doing so shame the hero into joining her—perhaps too late.

If the hero accepts the course of action because he does not recognize it as a threat, he will balk sometime during the course of action, as soon as the threat to his flaw becomes apparent.

Hero and ally instigate the first action against the opponent

Whatever the hero's initial response is—immediate balking or immediate acceptance of the course of action, the next step is *the hero and ally instigating the first action against the opponent.*

Opponent counterattacks and states his POV, Hero's ally reacts to balk

Then the opponent counterattacks, and in the process, the opponent clearly states his point of view.

Depending on when the hero balks—before or during the hero and ally's first action against the opponent, or perhaps during the opponent's counterattack, the balk will cause the hero's ally to react.

The ally might react angrily, certainly with some degree of surprise and confusion. Remember, the ally does not know about the hero's character flaw. The ally does not understand *why* the hero is balking.

It is up to you to choose when the hero's balk occurs. However, it is most powerful to have it occur during the hero and ally's first action against the opponent, or during the opponent's first counterattack. This is where the greatest jeopardy and therefore tension and drama exist.

For instance, our own hero and ally (the cowardly ex-green beret and the company president) might formulate a plan to use the company computers and the hero's computer skills (remember, he's an accountant) to track down the opponent. In the process they alert the computer-savvy opponent, who sends his thugs after the hero and the hero's ally. At the moment of confrontation, the hero freezes. It is only because of the hero's ally's actions that they escape.

This is a dramatic and exciting way to show the hero being hindered by his character flaw. It's also a great way to *trigger a response by the opponent*, which is the next step. It also gives the hero's ally a logical reason to tear into the hero. And, it also pushes the hero very strongly in the direction of choosing between his flaw and some other opportunity—such as the opportunity to regain his self-respect. It will, at the very least, pressure the hero into at least admitting he *has* a character flaw and that it might be hindering him.

Ally confronts hero about balk

At this point the hero's ally will confront the hero about his balking, and will either present an ultimatum or simply refuse to work with the hero's ally anymore, depending on how much the hero's ally needs and/or wants the hero. The hero's ally will certainly not want to go through such a balk again (*especially* if it involved danger).

CHAPTER EIGHTEEN

THE HERO STARTS GROWING

Hero renews his determination to meet the lifechanging event

At this point the hero will be forced to either give up the opportunity that's presented by the lifechanging event (if possible) and/or be willing to confront the opponent and to try to reconcile with the hero's ally. This means that the hero will have to renew his determination to meet the challenge of the lifechanging event and try to take advantage of the opportunity.

In our example, the company president's reaction will depend on how she feels about the hero—he could have been just another employee, or he could have been someone she was platonically fond of, or even someone she was attracted to. The hero can show his good qualities in his relationship with his boss, and she can respond by liking him, but being somewhat put off by her character flaw, which expresses itself in his meekness.

The hero's ally confronts our hero for having risked their lives with his balk, and she refuses to trust him anymore. She leaves him behind as she goes on by herself, trying to track down and confront the opponent. The hero learns that the hero's ally has gone on without him, placing her in danger, and he is shamed into going after her, with renewed determination. Now it's not just his own welfare that he's trying to protect, but the welfare of someone else, someone he cares about.

Hero expands his area of concern

This is the first instance of the hero expanding his area of concern. There may be other instances—the expansion can take place in several steps. For example, we can have the hero and hero's ally discover that the opponent plans to use the stolen money to buy a bomb to kill a bunch of people. This may be too much, but it certainly does raise the jeopardy dramatically, and forces the hero to expand his area of concern just as dramatically.

Or, it can be simpler—the hero begins by expanding his area of concern to include the hero's ally, and later expands it to include the other employees, who stand to lose everything they own because of the theft of their pension funds, IRAs, 401ks, whatever.

Hero confronts his character flaw

This is an important point in the story, because it is the first time that the hero confronts his character flaw, the first time he consciously, *willingly* decides to try to overcome it, despite the dangers involved, even if they're only emotional dangers.

Hero convinces ally to give him another chance

The script will be far too short and unexciting, however, if the hero completely overcomes his character flaw at this point. Instead, he needs to first convince the hero's ally to give him another chance. Second, he needs to take the next physical step against the opponent, and in so doing be able to prove himself to the hero's ally, and to begin to handle his character flaw.

So, our hero catches up to the hero's ally, and tries to get her to give him a second chance. She may or may not agree, but if she does, you know she's going to be tentative about it, mistrustful of this cowardly hero who has once before let her down and put her in danger.

CHAPTER NINETEEN

THE HERO TAKES ACTION

Hero proves himself to ally

The next step is for our hero to prove his renewed determination and trustworthiness to the hero's ally by taking responsibility for the next step against the opponent. This is going to be the first concrete step in shedding his character flaw—the first of several steps that occur on the way to the final confrontation.

In "Rocky," the hero takes several steps beginning with enlisting the help of a hero's ally (Burgess Meredith), agreeing to let Talia Shire move in (commitment to a second hero's ally), doing roadwork to get his conditioning up, punching the hell out of sides of beef (which also acts as a great metaphor for how he feels about herself—he's just a side of beef), allowing Burgess Meredith to teach him boxing technique, and finally running to the top of a huge set of stairs in Philadelphia at top speed to demonstrate his newly acquired conditioning and physical capabilities.

In our script, those steps taken by the hero may entail performing increasingly dangerous acts in the course of tracking down the opponent—but they have to be dangerous in context of the hero's character flaw. Simply climbing a building is not going to do it, because that has nothing to do with the point of origin.

The point of origin of the hero's character flaw had to do with the hero being trapped in an enclosed space by an enemy, with no way out, losing one ally after another, until the hero finally snapped, costing the lives of at least one of his remaining allies. This is what happened at the point of origin, when the hero, as a green beret, caused the death of his men by panicking and ordering an untimely retreat under fire. We need to remember this, because the danger the hero forces himself to face should have some relevance to that earlier danger which he failed to master. We and he should be reminded of that earlier danger in a very haunting, taunting way, so that we automatically wonder with dread whether the hero can do better than he did last time he faced danger of this kind.

Hero partially redeems himself, bonds with ally

This act of beginning to handle his character flaw gains the hero some redemption, some "brownie points" with the hero's ally. The hero's ally, mollified, bonds with the hero, realizing that the hero has a character flaw but that he is at least willing to try to overcome it.

Hero reveals part of his character flaw to ally

The ally also realizes that the hero's flaw is something extremely difficult for the hero to overcome. She offers some help to him, or at least give him a listening ear, and he accepts partially, revealing part of his character flaw, and the reason behind it, but then draws back. It's still too early for him to completely overcome his character flaw.

Ally makes demand of hero

This is also the point at which the still tentative hero's ally will make demands of the hero. She may demand that if she is to trust him and allow him to come along, he must open up to her, which is the subjective demand. She may demand that he let her lead the way (since she still doesn't trust him to do so).

The ally taking control can make the ally a positive role model for our hero. He sees how *does* take control and command (something he's afraid of doing, which is understandable, given what happened last time he did so).

Ally reveals her own struggles

This acting as a role model can be made more powerful if the hero's ally reveals something about herself that makes her being a role model more admirable. For example, she may reveal that she has had her own traumas and bad experiences which make taking command as difficult for her as it might be for the hero. This allows the hero to realize that he is not alone in his fears and difficulties. This puts things into perspective for our hero.

Think of the character flaw as a suit of armor. Yes, it protects the hero in some ways from having to face his past, and the pain therein. But the lifechanging event is like a flood that threatens to drown him. The danger of drowning is now actually increased by the very device that had earlier seemed like a protective device—the suit of armor. Remember, this is the function of the lifechanging event—to magnify the negative consequences of having the character flaw. That suit of armor was always heavy to carry around, but now that heaviness can kill our hero.

The hero, still in his suit of armor, responds to the lifechanging event by beginning to shed the suit of armor, but does so by taking off the smallest parts of it first, so as to hang on to as much protection as he can, for as long as he can. Maybe he takes off an armored boot first, because at least that way his heart is still protected.

Maybe he'll take off a chain mail glove, and maybe even, eventually, his helmet, but still he retains his torso armor so that his heart, at least, will remain protected.

Then, at some point, he has to make the final commitment, in order to stave off drowning. He casts off the last piece of armor (character flaw). In so doing, he is able to float to the surface, free of the deadweight. Free, also, to do battle with the opponent who caused the flood to begin with.

In "Rocky," Rocky Balboa begins his response to the lifechanging event by beginning to do roadwork. This is the easiest, least painful part of overcoming his character flaw—he can still be a loser as he runs through the streets. But, with each added action—accepting Burgess Meredith's help, learning new footwork and punching, allowing cameras to tape him beating up the sides of beef, he gives up more and more important parts of his image of being a loser.

Hero and ally unite against opponent

Okay, now begins a series of actions by the hero and hero's ally, who are now united, no longer at odds. These actions bring the hero closer to a confrontation with the opponent, a confrontation that resembles the original challenge. This will become the hero's chance to make a new, redefining, decision.

As the physical, objective steps are taken, steps have to be taken on the subjective, personal level as well, to prepare the hero to make a different decision than the one he made in the past.

One way would be for our hero to become more and more intimate (not necessarily *romantically* intimate) with the hero's ally, growing to care enough about her to want to include her in his area of concern.

The combination, then, is: a growing affection and/or respect for the hero's ally; a desire to earn the hero's ally's respect, and; a realization that the hero's ally has already done something similar to what the hero is afraid to do.

In "Rocky," Stalone lets Talia Shire ever deeper into his life, even to the point of having her move in with him. He comes to respect her more as he sees her fight her own battles and actually win those battles. She changes before his eyes, denying her brother's claim that she is a loser, changing her appearance, becoming more confident. She is a perfect role model for Rocky.

The goal is to make gaining the ally's respect more important to the hero than maintaining his character flaw. Alternatively, you can view it as making it just too humiliating for the hero to maintain his character flaw in the face of the ally's strength.

In larger terms, then, the goal is to make the character flaw smaller in importance to the hero than is the hero's ally. This, while taking steps toward finding and confronting the opponent.

Here's an idea: the hero is both an accountant and a risk-taker. After he knocks out the hoods who try to steal payroll from him, he goes to an extreme sports park where he rock-climbs, hang-glides, does obstacle courses—whatever, which shows us his extreme physical abilities. Then, at the end of this display of physical prowess, the hero is confronted by someone else at the park. The hero backs down, so that we're once again reminded of his character flaw. But we now have an interesting context to place that fear in: the context of the hero's amazing physical abilities.

Let's build this up even more. What if, during the original incident at the point of origin, our hero was the *commander* of the small squad of Green Berets trapped by the enemy. His decision to retreat got his men killed. He thereafter defined himself as a coward.

Maybe the hero, at the point of origin, ordered his men to try to break out and retreat, and in the process they were all slaughtered, except for the hero. And even though it was a well-meant order, the hero still sees it as an act of cowardice that cost his men their lives. Maybe this could be exacerbated by the fact that within a hour of the men getting killed, reinforcements arrived. If our hero had waited, his men would still be alive.

So, because our hero has this combination of computer savvy, physical prowess, military know-how and command experience, he is not only *willing* to help himself and the other employees, he is *able* to. However, he may still be willing to take this risk only for the *ally's* sake—his area of concern is larger, but still not as large as it could be.

So the hero organizes a combination "sting" and "commando" operation, in which he uses the computer eggheads in the company's accounting division to set up a computer sting operation. Meanwhile he simultaneously organizes his friends from the extreme sports park into a paramilitary unit to invade the opponent's headquarters or company.

The opponent is also a computer whiz. He's already seen the hero's ally and hero try to track him down using computers. So the hero knows that the opponent will be ready for them to try another computer attack. The hero also knows that the opponent may *not* be expecting to have to fend off a *physical* assault, especially since the opponent thinks of the hero as being a coward, and of the hero's ally of being "just a woman."

So the hero sets his accounting/computing team to perform a frontal computer assault on the opponent's computer system, while he leads his extreme sports team on a physical raid of the opponent's offices: "The Sting" meets "Sneakers" meets "Dirty Dozen." There's going to be ample chance here for the hero to come up against his character flaw. If he led his men to death at the point of origin, imagine the risk he is taking in organizing another team of men on a similarly dangerous mission.

In fact, to make the mission even more dangerous, lets make the opponent a mobster, a casino owner who has stolen the hero's ally's money and electronically merged it with his own casino's finances in order to avoid being killed by his mobster bosses for having lost a huge amount of money from the casino.

The "sting" part of the operation could be to sucker the opponent into making a mistake that gets him into trouble with his mob bosses. The risk to the hero, of course, is that this *is* the mob—not someone you want to mess with. Also, the casino may be on Indian land, and may be isolated, increasing the difficulty of physically breaking into the building.

No need to get into specifics here, but the point is that the hero undertakes to combine his own skills and those of his accounting and adrenalyn-junkie friends in an extremely risky assault on the opponent's stronghold in a combination sting operation/commando raid that carries the risk of his screwing up again, with lives on the line—again.

By the way, there's going to have to be some kind of justification for why the hero's ally and hero don't just call the cops. It could be a lack of proof, perhaps collusion between the opponent and the cops. It doesn't matter what it is, as long as it believably makes it necessary for the hero's ally and hero to take action on their own.

You can even throw in some kind of twist. What if the hero's ally was actually, secretly, the opponent's lover, who had planned to loot her own company with the opponent, but then was betrayed by the opponent at the last moment. This is why she turned to the hero, hoping to play on his "niceness" and his computer skills to help her recover the money.

This could be something that the hero discovers at the very end when the hero's ally turns on him. Or maybe it's something he has to get over in order to be able to trust and work with the ally to get the company's money back. Either way would work. An example of this kind of scenario is "The Verdict" with Paul Newman, in which the woman he falls in love with turns out to be a spy for the opposing attorneys.

Hero expands his area of concern even wider

By now it's become clear that the hero has expanded his area of concern even wider, to include not just the hero's ally, but now all of the men he has organized to attack the opponent, and all of the employees of the company, because by now the hero's ally has helped him realize what is at stake and who is at risk.

CHAPTER TWENTY

THE OPPONENT STRIKES BACK

Opponent countering hero and ally, the unravelling

And in the process of this, the opponent is countering each of the hero and ally's actions, the stakes, jeopardy and tension rising steadily on an objective level.

Now comes the unraveling—and at the perfect moment, because the hero has the most to lose. In fact the hero has as much to lose now as he had at the point of origin. This makes this an opportunity for him to react in either the same manner as he did at the point of origin (and thus perpetuate his flaw), or perhaps in a different manner that might allow him to redeem himself and resolve his flaw.

Opponent increasing area of threat

The opponent increases his area of *threat* just as the hero has expanded his area of *concern*. The two are definitely related. The hero starts to lose his men—maybe not literally. Maybe they get trapped in the casino, cut off, bound to be found out because there is a ticking clock: the hero's team have to be out by a certain time or else be discovered. And suddenly the hero is right back at the point of origin, leading a team of men into a trap, then having to decide what to do to save them, while the threat increases, and everything depends on his making the right decision.

Hero breaks his own rules

The hero often responds to the pressure by doing something that runs counter to his own rules of conduct and morality, in a desperate bid to defeat the opponent. It is at this moment that the hero and opponent are most alike, with one exception: the hero is breaking his own rules, but the opponent is actually *following* his own rules—same actions, different rules. The important thing here is that the "immoral" act that the hero performs or attempts to perform *does not work*. And that leaves him apparently defeated, because if breaking his own rules of conduct is a last resort, and even this fails, he is completely lost—or so it seems.

Opponent performs act forcing hero to completely abandon his flaw

The opponent now has all of the hero's men in danger, trapped in the casino, and the hero has seemingly blown his last chance. We can escalate the danger even more now, by having the opponent perform an act that must be responded to but that cannot be responded to without the hero completely abandoning his flaw.

What can that act be? Well, what if the opponent locks everyone—his own men, the casino patrons, and the hero and his men, in the casino, along with a huge bomb that is big enough to completely destroy the casino and everyone in it—both guilty parties and innocent bystanders alike?

More, what if the opponent also puts the hero's ally in peril, by having planted a similar bomb in the ally's company headquarters building? The opponent is determined to eliminate anyone who might be able to track him down.

This might, admittedly, be overkill, but it's exciting overkill. Imagine the hero, trapped in the casino, cut off from the hero's ally, thinking that his greatest peril is that the opponent and/or the police will discover him in the casino vaults?

Hero learns true danger

Then the hero learns, in succession, that: there is a bomb that will kill him and his extreme-sport weekend warriors; that the bomb will also kill the opponent's own men; that the bomb will kill the innocent bystanders patronizing the casino and; a second bomb will kill his ally and all the company employees who he has assigned to try to break into the opponent's computer system? And the hero realizes that this is at least partly his fault, for having brought the extreme athletes, company employees and hero's ally into the battle with the opponent.

This is the point that we have been working toward during the entire script—the point at which the hero either has to completely abandon his flaw or else actually perish—physically or emotionally.

This is the low point for the hero in this story, the moment of greatest peril and also, paradoxically, the moment of greatest opportunity.

CHAPTER TWENTY-ONE

THE HERO GETS A SECOND CHANCE

Second circumstance, challenge, decision, self-definition and emotional state

Now, in rapid order, the hero undergoes a Second Circumstance, a Second Challenge, a Second Decision, a Second Self-Definition and a Second Emotional state which will lead to his completely overcoming his character flaw and adopting a new behavior to replaces the old behavior, which was, of course, cowardice.

In our example this can be as follows: the second circumstance and the *second challenge* is the attack on the casino that's trapped the hero and his team inside. This is equivalent to the original circumstance, in which the hero led his men in an attack during the war.

The second decision arises out of the need to save his men once they're trapped in the casino, which parallels the original decision which was to either fight or flee. This is actually a nice parallel, because in both the original circumstance and in this newer, second circumstance, the hero had already achieved a certain level of leadership, enough to lead his men into battle in the first place.

The challenge comes, though, when the hero has to find a way out of a seemingly hopeless decision. In the first circumstance, his decision was to flee under enemy fire, and it got his men killed. Now he's trapped in the casino, so we have to give him a way out, but it has to be a way out that seems impossible, suicidal, just as running away, exposing one's back to enemy fire seemed suicidal.

The choice is the same: wait in the casino (foxhole/bunker) hoping that someone will save them, or take a risk so great that it seems suicidal. The last time the hero made a choice, he was wrong. Can he overcome the paralysis that will surely grip him, can he make the same decision, and will it be the right one?

This decision results in a second self-definition, that of being courageous rather than cowardly, a leader instead of a loser. No greater courage could be required of a man than to make a decision that he knows once killed men who depended on him.

Finally, this leads to a *new emotional state*—determination, perhaps, and leadership: **our** hero, now determined to redeem himself and save his men, acts decisively, as a leader, which is his *new behavior*—courage.

Final expansion of hero's area of concern

This is the final overcoming of the hero's character flaw and enabling circumstances and of everything that originally led up to that expression and circumstance. It's also the hero's final expansion of his area of concern.

An example of the kind of scenario that would fill these requirements: the hero and his men are trapped in the casino vault area. There is perhaps one way out, but it is blocked by a number of casino security guards, the opponent's militiamen followers. The hero realizes he is in the same situation, and he freezes.

Another of the extreme athletes, frustrated by the hero's inaction, takes matters in his own hands and decides to try to brave the security guard's fire in order to escape. At the last second, the hero comes to the extreme athlete's rescue, barely saving him from being killed.

The hero has had to make his decision, and though they are still trapped within the casino vaults, now, at least, the hero has thrown his hat into the ring. He doesn't know how he's going to get his men out, but now, finally, he is determined to use his considerable skills and leadership ability to do so.

Now we're ready for the *3rd and final act.*

SECTION SIX
THE THIRD ACT

CHAPTER TWENTY-ONE

THE BATTLE BEGINS BADLY

The 3rd act is the culmination of the hero's 2nd act struggle to: (a) find the opponent, (b) catch the opponent, or (c) to get ready to meet the opponent in battle (to train).

Examples of this third act are the final fight scene in "Rocky," and the dinner scene in "Secrets and Lies." There is no more time for "steps" leading up to *anything*. The hero is now already on the *top* step, and is sharing that narrow step with the opponent who is trying with all of his might to knock the hero off the step and to his (physical or emotional) death.

All or nothing

It's all or nothing, and it should *feel* like all or nothing, winner-take-all. The stakes are at their highest, the jeopardy, tension, conflict and drama should be at their peak. This act should have the feel of a rush to finality.

Damage to hero mounts

In this act, the damage to the hero mounts (emotionally and/or physically). The decision hangs in the balance. We should not know who wins until the final moments of the film—unless there is a "tag" scene at the end, which can be used to tie up loose ends.

So let's back up a bit and recap. The hero set his accounting/computer whizzes to do an electronic frontal assault on the opponent's computer system. As a back-up plan, and/or diversion, the hero takes his troop of extreme athletes into the casino with him, to try to *physically* recover the stolen money from the casino vaults.

The hero and his troops "stealth" their way into the casino, while the accountant computer geeks attack electronically.

Something goes wrong. The hero and his troops are trapped inside. The hero and his men then discover that instead of a few million dollars in gambling cash, the casino has *billions* of of dollars in both cash and securities and in electronic deposits, linked to banks around the world. This is bigger and more dangerous than they could ever have imagined.

The accountant/geeks are able to manipulate the computer-operated security system just enough to keep the casino guards from knowing that the hero and his men are inside the vault area of the casino. But the hero and his men are cut off from communicating with the hero's ally or anyone else.

Now the truth about the casino becomes clear: it is the headquarters for a national militia group of unbelievable proportion. The militia has stolen huge amounts of money and stockpiled it over a period of years. Their intention is to use the money to destabilize the economy, and take over the government surreptitiously, by bankrupting both political parties, and blackmailing politicians and financial leaders.

This is the final expansion of the hero's area of concern. The story began as his attempt merely to save or rescue his own enabling circumstances—his pension funds and his job. It became a concern for the company president, then for the other employees, then his troop of extreme athletes, and now, finally, for the entire country.

We can add one more jeopardy here that might add more concreteness and immediacy to the danger—the casino clients come into danger. The casino is filled with clients. The head of the militia has set a huge explosive device meant to destroy the casino and all the other militia members, the opponent having arranged for all his militia followers to be in the casino for a meeting.

The opponent has suckered everybody. He has billions of dollars he's about to transfer to Swiss banks. He'll then blow up the casino with all the militia personnel, casino employees and patrons, to make it look as if some rival militia group set off the explosion. Meanwhile the opponent plans to sneak off to Europe with his fortune and a new identity, with no surviving militia members to share the booty or track him down.

The low point

This is the low point for the hero. The opponent seals off the casino, locking the militiamen, casino patrons and the hero and his team inside with the bomb. Then the opponent sets off for the airport.

CHAPTER TWENTY-THREE

THE HERO FIGHTS BACK

Hero discovers a way to fight back

It seems hopeless. There is no way out for the hero and the others in the fortified, locked-up casino. Then, the hero finds or learns something, something that gives him a chance—a small chance, perhaps, but a chance.

Audience discovers full extent of opponent's threat

Just, however, as the hero learns or finds what he *thinks he needs, the audience (but not the hero) learns something else—the audience learns the full extent of the opponent's threat,* something new that ups the danger even more, and that the hero needs to know or else he's going to lose and/or perish.

What this step does is amp up the tension tremendously. Imagine, as an audience member, that you've just seen the opponent's second gun, but the hero hasn't. You know that unless the hero learns about the "second gun," he will be destroyed by the opponent. This drives you crazy is a very exciting way.

Say, for instance, that our hero learns that there is a way out—a ventilation crawlway, a door stuck away in some unnoticed area of the vault—whatever. What he doesn't know, though, is that the opponent rigged the door to detonate as soon as the hero gets the door open. WE, the audience, know about the bomb, the hero doesn't, and as he reaches for the door, we're holding our breath.

Back to our own story. Okay, our hero is stuck in the casino. There's a bomb planted that will kill everyone. There is no apparent way out. The hero is cut off from the outside world. Then, for a few brief moments, he is put into communication with the hero's ally—a cell phone works for a few moments of static-marred words, and the hero's ally is able only to say that she has alerted the police/FBI and that they are on their way. Then the phone goes dead again.

Now, the hero is right back to where he was years before. He is responsible for a band of people he is leading. There is the threat of death at their doorstep, about to explode any second. Help is on the way, but the casino is so isolated that there's no telling how long it'll take to get there. Does the hero hold on, hoping that the help gets there before the bomb goes off? Does the hero take a major risk to get his people out of harm's way? And remember, the last time he made this decision, he got a lot of people killed.

Then things get even worse—the hero discovers a possible way out, but it is so dangerous that it is very much like the danger involved in trying to flee to safety by placing one's back to enemy fire. But now, at least, the hero has a real choice, and he decides to take the chance.

Then we, the audience make our little discovery about the full threat that the opponent presents. So, our hero has found some form of possible, though extremely dangerous escape. We, the audience now see the bomb (literal or figurative) on the other side of that possible escape route, set to go off.

Hero learns of increased threat

Then, finally, just before it can destroy him, the hero discovers what we already know about the opponent's true threat, the bomb or other threat lying on the other side of the door/escapeway that is the only chance of escape.

CHAPTER TWENTY-FOUR

FINAL BATTLE

Hero fully engages opponent

Now the hero knows the real and complete danger. It's daunting, but at least he now knows what he's dealing with, and he makes his plan accordingly. Though in our story the hero does not engage the opponent directly, he does fully engages the opponent's guards and militiamen, and the traps left by the opponent.

The hero handles the physical task of getting out of the casino and/or defusing the bomb, while the company president uses her computer geeks to track the money being transferred to Switzerland, or maybe to retrieve it from Switzerland, while also trying to track the opponent electronically—through credit cards, taxi services, airline reservations.

This can become a great scene if the opponent foresaw the possibility of being tracked and created a spider web of identities and tickets so that the company president has to track down every lead, frantically trying to find out which is the real one, trying to alert the police at the same time. We can intercut between the hero trying to get out alive, the opponent trying to escape, and the hero's ally trying to track the opponent down through a web of ATMs, credit card receipts, etc. Meanwhile the computer geeks are trying to track down the billions the opponent has deposited in Swiss banks.

Hero restates point of view

Somewhere in here, though, we need a couple of other elements: the opponent needs to reaffirm his point of view, and the hero needs to reaffirm his, in the fact of the opponent's point of view. Since the hero does not directly engage the opponent, we can do this by proxy: the opponent's second-in-command is a woman who passionately believes in the militia movement and its supposed ideals as set up by the opponent. She does directly oppose the hero as he tries to escape, and she also represents something like what the hero once thought he could be: a fanatically loyal patriot willing to risk her life for her beliefs.

Opponent restates point of view

So the opponent's proxy, the second in command, is the one that the hero engages, and who espouses the opponent's pov. But let's add something even more: while the hero is battling the second-in-command to try to get out alive without setting off the bomb, the opponent is fleeing, taking a cab to the airport, maybe stopping off at a bank to arrange a last-minute transfer of funds, whatever. And as he flees, he begins to be haunted by the full impact of what he is doing—the mass murder he is about to commit not only against his innocent enemies, but against his own people, people who have trusted him with their very lives.

This could be a fascinating and ironic way of showing how similar and yet different the opponent is from the hero: the opponent has gotten screwed somehow in the past, and thought he could use that to justify his actions. But the father he gets from the casino and the closer to freedom, the more he becomes like the hero, a man overwhelmed by guilt for what he has set in motion, the lives that will be destroyed by his actions. And as we see him start to crumble, we can contrast that with the hero, who has somehow found the courage and redemption he never thought he could have.

Hero defeats or is defeated by opponent

Depending on whether this is a tragedy as in "Macbeth" or "Leaving Las Vegas," the hero will at this point complete the struggle against the opponent by either defeating or being defeated by the opponent.

The upshot is that the hero cannot disarm the bomb, but does find a way out, and gets everyone out before the bomb goes off. Meanwhile the geeks and company president track down both the money and the opponent, retrieving the money and having the FBI arrest the opponent at the airport.

Then the hero gets to a phone and calls the company president. She successfully evacuates her own building just before it is destroyed by the blast. At this point they can live happily ever after.

Or, if we've decided on the twist of her having been the opponent's lover and accomplice, we can either have her arrested, or perhaps the hero can forgive her. Or maybe she doesn't get arrested, but the hero walks away from her in disgust or simply from a brokenhearted realization that as much as he loves her, he'll never be able to trust her.

Now there are several other things you might also want to accomplish in this third act, that are not included in the aforementioned description of our little story. These include:

- the hero engaging the opponent
- the opponent reaffirming his point of view
- the hero reaffirming his pov
- the opponent denigrating the hero's point of view
- the opponent pointing out the hero's culpability
- the hero admitting to his culpability and yet still restating his point of view

- one point of view emerging triumphant subjectively
- one character emerging triumphant objectively
- the hero changing, and facing the future as a changed person.

A lot of this is going to be accomplished during the hero's confrontation either with the opponent or the opponent's proxy, the second-in-command. Someone once said that an argument (or confrontation) is nothing but an exchange of values. So it is here with the hero and opponent (or proxy). As they battle, the opponent should reaffirm his point of view—after all, the clash in their points of view is what this is all about. If they were both of the same point of view, they'd be allies, not opponents.

The opponent denigrates the hero's point of view—he might tell the hero that he is a loser because he keeps letting himself be ruled by conscience and guilt and obedience to the "rules." The opponent feels that he has won because he's willing to do whatever is necessary to win. In stating his point of view, the opponent can also denigrate the hero's point of view.

The hero can reply by reaffirming his belief that he owed it to himself and to his men to try to save them, rather than to run away and betray them, as the opponent has decided to do to his own men.

At this point the opponent can point out the hero's culpability: the opponent would never have been able to do what he has done if the hero hadn't been too afraid to try to stop him. This is the old Edmund Burke quote: "all is takes for evil to triumph is for good men to do nothing." We could set this up by giving the hero a chance early in the script to find out what the opponent is really up to, but have him be afraid to become involved.

The hero must admit to his culpability here, or else he really hasn't completely overcome his flaw. But, the hero uses his own culpability as the very reason he is sticking to his point of view—he needs to make amends for his culpability. This is the point at which the hero's and opponent's points of view are most clearly and strongly stated, and *one of those points of view emerges triumphant.* In this case, we may see the hero's point of view emerge triumph more gradually, as we watch the opponent begin to disintegrate during his attempt to flee, while the hero's ally electronically hunts him down.

This philosophical and emotional conflict greatly deepens and makes more meaningful the mere physical conflict between the hero and opponent. It's also why we need to know a lot about the hero and opponent. If we had known absolutely nothing about Rocky Balboa and Apollo Creed, the final boxing match at the end of the movie would have been far less meaningful and even, perhaps, completely meaningless.

Once the opponent leaves the casino, then, the hero continues to struggle against him, in the form of the traps the opponent has set, and the bombs he has left behind, both at the casino and at the company headquarters. The hero does manage to save his men as well as the casino patrons and even, ironically, the opponent's men.

Then the hero races to the company headquarters and saves the company president and other employees, as the company president causes the opponent to be nailed—one character has emerged triumphant objectively.

CHAPTER TWENTY FIVE

EPILOG

Hero, changed by the events in the story, faces the future

The hero now faces the future as a very different person.

Optional final twist

There is, in fact, one more step that can be taken that can intensify the third act tremendously. When the hero breaks into the casino, he can discover evidence that the hero's ally is actually aligned with the opponent. The opponent can then use this fact in his confrontation with the hero, taunting him for his desire to do the "right thing" when even his own ally isn't doing the right thing.

This twist raises the emotional stakes of the final battle, and also lends a certain edge to the whole act. This is especially so if we learn the truth about the ally *before* the hero learns it. We'll then be sitting on the edge of our seats, dreading the moment when the hero finds out, and also wanting him to find out before he makes a possibly fatal error based on his mistaken belief that the ally is on his side.

SECTION SEVEN
THE NEXT STEP

CHAPTER TWENTY SIX

CREATING A BLUEPRINT

An outline or treatment

The next step is to put all of the aforementioned steps into the form of a summary that you can use to either pitch your story to a producer or agent, or to use as a blueprint for the actual writing of your story. The easiest way to do this is to use a single sentence for each of the elements, and then to edit the result down to a point at which it concisely conveys the gist of the story in what are sometimes called "plot points."

Plot point outline

- In the middle of a battle, JACK, the leader of a squadron of elite special services soldiers, orders a retreat that results in the death of his men, leading him to define himself as a coward.

- After the war, Jack seeks out the safest job he can find, becoming an accountant for a mid-sized company. He creates a nice, safe world in which he will never be asked to do anything that might reveal his cowardice. He maintains a meek, unassuming demeanor, though he keeps his physical skills honed through rigorous exercise and participation in a weekend "extreme sports" group he belongs to that does rock climbing, martial arts, sky diving etc.

- Jack is sweet on LESLIE, the president of the company that Jack works for. Jack, however, feels too badly about himself to approach Leslie romantically.

- Leslie is attracted to Jack, but put off by his overt meekness.

- BART is a company VP who fawns on Leslie and belittles Jack.

- When asked about Bart's abuse, Jack merely states that it's Jack's job to follow Bart's orders because Bart is his superior. Bart overhears Jack's feeble explanation, and tears into him, claiming that you take what you can when you can, because it's dog-eat-dog. Bart reveals that his father was destroyed by the "system" and that he, Bart, was never going to let that happen to him.

- We see Jack's conflicting personality traits when he is asked to make the "night deposit" of company funds, something he's never done before. Arriving at the bank, Jack is jumped by a gang of muggers. For a few moments, Jack the accountant becomes Jack the Green Beret, and he lashes out, beating up all the muggers. Then, however, he suddenly bolts in panic, giving in once more to his fear.

- Bart uses computers to electronically loot the company's bank accounts and pension plans. He then disappears, leaving the company in danger of folding, and thus threatening the jobs, pensions and life savings of the employees.

- Jack, realizing his safe world is in danger, reluctantly teams up with Leslie, to try to track Bart down. Bart lashes out. Jack freezes in fear, nearly getting himself and Jane killed. Only Leslie's quick thinking saves them.

- Leslie rejects Jack for nearly getting them killed with his cowardice.

- Jack, humiliated, learns that Leslie has gone on alone to try to find Bart. For the first time, the shame of Jack's cowardice is outweighed by the need to redeem himself.

- Jack catches up with Leslie and convinces her to give him another chance. She is reluctant to do so, still angry with Jack, especially since she does not know the real reason for his cowardice, and cannot trust him.

- To prove himself, Jack puts himself at risk to try to locate Bart, which mollifies Leslie. She bonds with Jack, who reveals a part of the reason for his cowardice.

- Jack discovers that Leslie has her own ghosts and fears, and he is inspired by the fact that she has the courage to go on despite them.

- Jack uses Leslie as a role model to bolster his own courage, and also develops stronger feelings for her, based on his admiration for her.

- Jack risks herself even further to find out that Bart owns a casino/resort in the desert.

- Lacking proof of Bart's culpability, Jack and Leslie are unable to get the authorities to help them.

- Though not completely at peace with his own demons, Jack organizes the company's computer geeks/accountants into an electronic strike force to try to break into Bart's casino-based computer system to recover the money.

- Jack realizes how much is at stake for the company's other employees, and that he represents not only his own interests, and Leslie's safety, but also the interests, jobs and life savings of every company employee. Their lives will be shattered unless the money is recovered.

- When the company's computer geeks discover that it is going to be a lengthy procedure to break into the casino's computers, Jack organizes a team of fellow adrenalyn-junkies who jump at the chance to put their war-game skills to real use by breaking into the casino to rob it of the equivalent amount of money that Bart stole from the company.

- While the computer geeks/accountants keep trying to break into the casino's computers, Jack leads his weekend "extreme sports" warriors in a break-in of Bart's casino. They skillfully bypass the casino's unusually heavy security to get into the casino's vaults.

- Jack and his men become trapped in the casino's vaults when the casino's much heavier *secondary* security system locks them in.

- Jack discovers that the casino's huge vaults are actually the headquarters for a huge militia that has stolen billions of dollars and placed it in banks around the world. Unless they can get out by a certain time, Jack and his weekend warriors will be discovered and killed by Bart's casino security force.

- Bart, in order to tie up loose ends, plants a bomb in Leslie's company building, a bomb that will destroy the building and everyone in it.

- Jack learns of Bart planting the bomb in the company building, then learns that Bart has also planted a bomb in the casino, intending to kill Jack, Jack's men, Bart's militiamen, and the casino patrons. Bart plans to flee to Europe where he has billions hidden in various banks. Then Jack discovers proof that Leslie has been Bart's accomplice, and that Bart is double-crossing her too.

- Bart seals off the entire casino, trapping everyone inside, and sets off for the airport.

- Jack begins breaking his men out of the casino vaults, while Leslie, not knowing there is a bomb in her own building, begins electronically tracking Bart's escape and the money that Bart has transferred to various bank accounts in Europe.

- Jack breaks free of the casino vaults and gets everyone out of the casino just in time to watch the casino be destroyed in a massive explosion.

- Leslie finds Bart's money—all of it, not just what he's stolen from her company, and transfers it back to her own accounts.

- Leslie electronically tracks Bart and has him arrested at the airport.

- Jack desperately calls Leslie, who evacuates her building just in time to avoid the blast that destroys the building completely.

- Jack turns Leslie over to the police for her having been Bart's accomplice.

OR: Jack embraces Leslie, having forgiven her because she helped capture Bart and return the money.

OR: Jack walks away from Leslie.

OR, it can be left ambiguous.

Is it Shakespeare?

Absolutely not. It may not even be decent "James Bond" or "Die Hard"—depending on how well it's executed. But it IS a story, one that can be tinkered with, expanded, changed, executed in a number of ways.

Glancing back at the story a second time (remember, this story was created from scratch as I went along, using the formula), I realize that what's missing from the story most of all is more emphasis on the theme, though much of that will come out in the actual screenplay once it's written.

This should be the story of a man seeking to find a reason to be courageous. He finds it when he discovers that he can't run from his cowardice, nor bury it nor lie about it, that eventually it all catches up to you, and in the meantime you're spending your time suffering in dread anticipation. "A hero dies but once, a coward dies a thousand deaths." Or, "what you resist persists."

This theme needs to be not only enunciated more clearly and strongly in this story, but also in a way that is relevant to the reader/viewer. Very few of us will identify with a cowardly Green Beret. However, we can identify with the story of a man who is afraid and who learns that he has to face those fears or suffer a fate even worse than whatever it is that caused him to have those fears in the first place.

Breaking the rules—or outgrowing them

You can break any number of rules, now that you know what those rules are, to achieve any kind of effect you want. Will you, years from now as a great screenwriter, be following the minutiae of this formula? I hope not, because I want you to have the confidence and imagination to run rampant. You'll still be using some of what's contained here, surely, even if it's only that you have a hero and opponent and hero's ally, and lifechanging event. But the point here is that by adhering to a formula, you can create for yourself the foundation not just of a good story, but of a good writing career.

Now, let's go on to what may be the most important chapter in the book.

CHAPTER TWENTY-SEVEN

HIGH CONCEPT

The most important chapter in this book

"High concept" is the most important phrase in Hollywood right now, and has been for many years. It simply means that the concept, the *premise* of your story is so strong that it can be captured in one or two sentences in a way that immediately intrigues the listener, and that seems unique, fresh, and pleasantly surprising. It means, in other words, that your premise is so unique and exciting that you can sell your story or at least seriously interest someone in your story using only the premise itself.

My friend's $600,000 high-concept story

The best recent example I've seen of a high concept story is that of a friend of mine who sold this script, the first he'd *ever* sold, for $600,000 within a day or so of it being sent out by his agent. The premise: "A calloused but successful radio psychologist about to get his own television show, starts suffering the neuroses of the patients he abuses on-air. He races to find a cure for his growing list of neuroses as he stutters, drools and twitches his way toward his first live television broadcast."

You can *see* this concept being played out. Imagine Jim Carey, Steve Martin, perhaps Robin Williams, taking on more and more neuroses, twitching, drooling, stuttering, shoplifting, drinking, sniffing glue, shouting out obscenities at inappropriate moments, picking his nose, exposing himself in public, getting worse and worse, completely out of control, avoiding the sponsors and producers of his upcoming television show, knowing that his own callousness has caused his problems, and knowing that somehow he's going to have to confront that flaw in order to cure himself in time to do the television show.

Add to that that the only reason he's successful is exactly the biting attitude that's gotten him into this mess in the first place. It's absolutely brilliant, and features a role that even the top Hollywood comic actors would fight for.

Can we quantify high concept?

The important question is: can we quantify "high concept?" Can we come up with principles that can help us create such high concepts for ourselves? Perhaps. Let's look at the elements that are common to high-concept movies.

CHAPTER TWENTY-EIGHT

THE HIGH CONCEPT FORMULA

The elements of high concept

After studying my friend's concept in particular, I've seen that it contains several crucial elements that make it work well.

First, it has a definite profession (it could just as well have been a situation rather than a profession) for the hero.

Second, it gives the hero a very definite flaw that is related to that profession. Being unsympathetic certainly causes problems and goes against the usual image of a psychologist.

Third, there is an event that forces the main character to choose between his flaw and some opportunity, in this case it's the opportunity to overcome the neuroses and to learn how to be empathetic to his radio patients.

Fourth, the idea is fresh.

Fifth, there is a strong sense of irony at play. It is extremely ironic that a psychologist starts exhibiting the neurotic behavior of his patients. It would not be ironic for a plumber to start exhibiting the neurotic behavior of his customers.

Analyzing my friend's story

Let's look at my friend's story one more time. What is the one problem that can happen to a psychologist that is strongly related to the fact that the hero IS a psychologist? How about he starts exhibiting the psychological problems of his patients? That's funny, but it needs one other thing: the fact that this also *has to do with his flaw*—that he is *abusing* those patients, and that taking on their neuroses *forces him to confront his flaw*. It also forces him to understand how painful those neuroses are, especially given that he has created a successful radio show by making *fun* of both the neuroses and the people who suffer them.

The problem must relate to both the hero's flaw and to who he is

So what's important here? That the problem relates to both the hero's flaw and to who he is. If the hero in my friend's story had been a dog groomer, it wouldn't have been as effective, because a story about a dog groomer who takes on the neuroses of his clients, doesn't make sense and doesn't make anyone laugh.

If the hero had been a really *empathetic, caring* psychologist, it wouldn't have been as effective, because there wouldn't have been as strong an irony or any connection to the hero's flaw. There's no irony to a really nice, caring psychologist suddenly taking on the neuroses of the patients he's trying so hard to help.

So, again, what we seem to have here are the following elements:

- a hero with a definite profession or situation
- a hero with a definite flaw that's *related* to his profession and/or situation

- an event that forces the main character to choose between his flaw and some opportunity that's related to his flaw *and* to his profession and/or situation
- freshness, uniqueness
- a sense of irony arising from the relationship between the event and the hero's profession or situation

Applying the elements

So, let's try to apply these elements and see if we can come up with a high concept right here and now. Let's pick a hero with a specific flaw that relates to who he is and/or what he does, and then find a problem that relates directly to *both* who he is and to his flaw, and that forces him to confront that flaw.

Let's be really random about this, just as an experiment. Let's go with the dog groomer we've already mentioned. Okay, we need an event that relates to both his profession and to his flaw. Let's say that he becomes a dog himself. Okay, at least that's relevant to what he does. Now we need to find a flaw that's relevant to both who/what he is, and to the event.

Let's say that the dog groomer has a lot going for him in his life, but he doesn't realize it, and he's quite bitter and jealous. In fact, he feels as if the dogs he grooms have a better life than he does, and one day he actually states that he'd rather be one of his wealthy clients' pets than a lowly dog groomer. SHAZAAM!! Our hero trades places with a wealthy client's horny male dog.

Now is this high concept? Can we state it clearly in a sentence or two? An unappreciative dog groomer accidentally change places with one of his rich clients' pampered pets—a horny but infertile pit bull who's facing castration unless he can impregnate a champion female pit bull. While the pit bull in the groomer's body eats raw meat, relieves himself in public, and humps sofas, dogs and every girl he can catch, the groomer faces either bestiality or castration, unless he can find a way back to his suddenly attractive human life.

Funny? Yes. Good comic potential? Yes. But it's not as good as my friend's story about the psychologist. Why? Because it takes too long to encapsulate the story, and because it's not unique enough. The Shaggy Professor comes to mind, though I'm sure there are also other examples of stories that make this one seem just too familiar. Does that mean this concept isn't viable? No. It just means that it's not as purely high concept as my friend's script.

Another high concept example

Try this: The President of the United States is infected with a germ warfare agent that forces him to tell the truth—and he's contagious!

This is the concept for "Truthies," a script I wrote years before "Bullworth," "Dave" or "Liar, Liar," but just didn't get around to pitching. It, like my friend's concept, is so easily conveyed in a single line, that it is obviously extremely high concept.

What's missing from our dog groomer story? For one thing, the close relationship between the flaw and the profession. Presidents lie, therefore it's funny and ironic that one of them be forced to tell the truth. Psychologists cure their patients, so it's funny that, instead of making his patients sane, a shrink's patients make him crazy.

What does a do groomer do? He grooms dogs. Being envious does not connect as strongly or naturally to being a dog groomer, as lying does to a politician, especially since the Clinton and Nixon fiascoes. There is also, by the way, something at least a little hateful about both of those professions: the know-it-all, manipulative, egghead shrinks who want to dissect us; the lying, manipulative politicians. In fact, "Liar, Liar" worked precisely because of the hero's profession—he was even worse than a politician, he was a lawyer! Imagine a lying, weasely lawyer being forced to tell the truth. Imagine a cold-hearted, arrogant psychologist himself suffering the symptoms of the poor people whose lives he holds in his uncaring hands.

What do we have against dog groomers? What strong characteristics—either positive or negative, do we associate with dog groomers? None, I suspect. Does this make it impossible for us to write a story about a dog groomer? No, and in fact the description of our dog groomer story attracts me enough to want to write that script, and I think I will. But if I'm looking for a one-sentence description of a story, a concept high enough to snag an executive/producer/agent's attention, "a dog groomer becomes a dog," doesn't do it.

So why does "A psychologist begins taking on his patient's symptoms" make it? Because we can immediately imagine the consequences in specific terms. "The President of the United States is infected with a virus that forces him to tell the truth—and he's contagious." This immediately brings to mind implications, problems, scenes, dialogue, humor, drama, irony.

There's that word again—irony. I think this is a big part of it, as is conflict. It may not be *humorously* ironic that a priest fall in love with a woman as happened in the hit miniseries and novel "Thorn Birds," but it is still ironic and filled with conflict and drama.

Again, "A priest falls in love" is all you need to imagine all sorts of scenes, problems, conflict. Why? Because the job description entails responsibilities that directly conflict with the event!

A psychologist is charged with curing neuroses. Taking on the neuroses of his patients directly conflict with the hero's responsibilities.

A priest is charged with caring for the *spiritual* needs of those around him, in a fatherly, asexually loving way that steers those people away from their baser instincts, including, in many instances, sex. Falling in love, indulging his own lust, runs directly counter to that responsibility.

We have come to see lawyers as the ultimate liars, an image only strengthened by the O.J. Simpson trial's Johnny Cochran and Robert Shapiro. We have also come to associate politicians with lying, again helped by Clinton, Nixon, Reagan, and so on.

To have either of these professions involved in being *forced* to tell of truth runs counter not, perhaps, to their responsibilities, but certainly to the qualities we have come to ascribe to these people. A priest telling the truth is not powerful, because we don't see it running counter to our image of what priests do. A priest falling madly in love with a beautiful woman *does* run counter to that image and immediately evokes images, scenes, dialogue, conflict.

That, then, is the most powerful element or quality of a high concept log line: that it is *immediately* evocative of what the story will be about. This is still not enough, though. Why? Because if the concept has been done before, you will have trouble selling it.

Although "Truthies" is extremely high concept, I waited too long to start pitching it to execs and agents. "Dave," "Liar, Liar" and, finally, "Bullworth" put "Truthies" in its grave. Suddenly "The President is infected with virus that forces him to tell the truth" is no longer evocative of anything unique, but rather evocative of other movies that are just too similar for "Truthies" to be any longer commercially viable.

What we have so far

So, what do we have so far in our search for a formula for creating high concept log lines?

a) We know that we need a hero whose job, profession, or situation in life involves certain very strong responsibilities or qualities (either positive or negative) that are general knowledge among the moviegoing public. For example, we don't associate any strong qualities to a dog groomer, but we do to politicians and lawyers.
b) We need an event to occur that runs completely counter to those responsibilities or qualities in a strong, dramatic and original way. A lawyer having to tell the truth, a priest falling in love.
c) We need the conflict between the event and the hero's qualities/profession to be strongly evocative of specific scenes, images, dialogue, problems, and so on. We can immediately see the problems that a smitten priest will face.
d) We need the event to be something unfamiliar and unexpected. A priest telling the truth is not unfamiliar or unexpected. A priest falling in love is, and has all sorts of interesting and dramatic implications to the hero.

Begin with the hero

So, let's begin with a hero who has a profession and/or position that carries responsibilities and/or qualities strongly ascribed to it by the general public. How about a priest who is asked by the devil to represent him in a law suit against God?

I know I jumped a step of two there, but I had to go with the inspiration. If we had been a little more methodical, we would have first decided upon a profession, such as priest. We then could have mulled over what kind of events would run counter to the responsibilities and/or reputation of a priest. "Thorn Birds" was about a priest falling in love with a woman, which certainly is high concept, counter to what we expect of priests.

What else runs counter to what we normally think of as a priest's responsibilities or reputation? A priest serves God. What if a priest was asked or even *forced* to serve *Satan* instead of *God*?

How you answer that question is going to depend on your particular imaginative bent. My own "flash" was in terms of the added oddity of a priest who was a lawyer—I'm guessing that the Vatican has its own lawyers, or at least legal experts, and that some of them are also priests. Of course, the very combination of lawyer and priest is funny or at least conflicting.

Evoke the second act

We're still missing something here, and that's the second act. When I said that a high concept log line would be evocative of scenes, ideas, dialogue and so on, I was really saying that the log line would be evocative of the second act. So far with this Priest/Devil log line, there is no second act.

The hero's flaw

Another thing we're missing is the hero's flaw. This is crucial, because unless the priest has some kind of flaw, the story's over before it starts—what priest is going to represent the Devil in any matter, much less in a law suit against God, unless there is some flaw that drives him to do it? Jim Carey's character in "Liar, Liar" was a liar, which is the only reason that his being forced to tell the truth is effective. It was his flaw, the lying, that made telling the truth interesting. Similarly, unless our lawyer/priest has a flaw, representing the devil is not in and of itself enough.

Let's say the priest is having a crisis in faith. Perhaps he's fallen in love, or perhaps he's been involved in some tragedy that's caused him to question the goodness of God—maybe a friend, family member or other loved one has died of cancer, or he's been part of some disaster so horrific that even someone as devout as him has reached the point of doubting his own faith in God.

Our high concept log line so far

Okay, so here's the log line: A darkly irreverent comedy in which a priest, driven to a crisis in faith by the suffering of the world, agrees to represent the Devil in a class action lawsuit against God, and ends up representing not Satan, but the people of Earth, and of heaven and of hell, all of whom cry out to know: "Is this all there is?"

CHAPTER TWENTY-NINE

"FIXING" LOW CONCEPT SCRIPTS

Reviewing the elements

Okay, I'm writing that screenplay as soon as I'm finished writing this book. In fact, depending on what edition of this book you're reading, I may have already written this screenplay. But in the meantime, let's review the elements of our newly created high concept formula:s

1) a hero whose profession, situation and/or reputation carries with it a lot of dramatic responsibilities and/or qualities attributed to that profession by the general public. For instance, the general public usually attributes lying to lawyers and politicians, and Godliness to priests.
2) a character flaw that runs counter to the responsibilities or qualities associated with the hero and/or his profession. For example, a priest whose flaw is that he's having a crisis in faith.
3) an event that magnifies the consequences of the hero's flaw to the point at which he will be destroyed in some way if he cannot overcome that flaw. If my friend's psychologist doesn't overcome his arrogance toward his patients, he will continue to suffer their neuroses and be destroyed as a psychologist.
4) conflict that immediately and strongly evokes specific scenes, conflict, drama and/or humor—and the second act. An uncaring psychologist starts taking on the neuroses of his patients.

5) freshness. Although an embittered dog groomer switching places with one of his client's dogs is high concept, it's not fresh enough. Body switching movies abound. "The Shaggy D.A." involved a human becoming a dog. Similarly, "Truthies" missed the boat on which "Dave," "Liar, Liar" and "Bullworth" sailed to success.

A note here: your screenplay doesn't *have* to be high concept. Some of the best movies ever made are not particularly high concept. "Forrest Gump" defies a log line. "Casablanca" is hard to pitch in just a line or two. "Trip to Bountiful," "Driving Miss Daisy," "Fargo," "Steel Magnolias" and "Postcards from the Edge" are all low-concept movies, and all of them are brilliant. However, high concept *does* make it easier to get a script read, especially for a newcomer.

It's like having a photo of that remote cabin you're trying to sell. If the potential buyer likes what he sees in the photo, he might be willing to travel to see the cabin itself. Similarly, if you can have a "photo" that captures the essence of the story in an interesting way, it might be attractive enough to entice an exec or agent into reading the actual script.

Can we turn low concept into high concept?

Okay, one last question: can we use our new high concept formula to not only create a high concept script, but also to turn a low-concept script into a high concept script? Let's find out.

I wrote a screenplay entitled "The Server." It was meant to be a big action piece, more commercial than the well-received but unsold screenplays I'd written before.

"The Server" is about an apathetic Gen-X process server who serves only delinquent Boomer dads, because his own father abandoned him when he was a child. One day someone hires him anonymously to find a particularly hard-to-find delinquent dad. Our hero finds the man in the company of two other men who are obviously cops of some kind. As our hero tries to serve the man, shots ring out, and the man and his two police companions fall dead. Our hero escapes, along with a beautiful female bystander, but both are then framed for the murders by the real killer: a terrorist who used our hero to find another terrorist who was about to tell the FBI about the terrorist leader's plan to set off a huge blast in L.A.

You can see the problem right away, I'm sure: it took me a paragraph to describe the concept, and even an entire paragraph didn't create any real excitement, surprise or humor. Let's see if we can change that so that *I* can sell "The Server" and *you* can understand the method by which you can create your own high concept and apply it to either a new script or to a script you may have already written but that you haven't been able to sell.

Okay, let's do this, once more step by step. We need the following:

1) a hero whose profession, situation and/or reputation carries with it a lot of dramatic responsibilities and/or qualities known and accepted by the general public.

Who is our hero? A process server. What responsibilities and/or qualities does the general public associate with that profession? None, unfortunately. This is our first roadblock. However, our hero is a Gen-xer, and we do associate certain qualities with "slackers," namely laziness, anti establishmentarianism, irresponsibility—the "Nintendo Generation."

Next, we need:

2) a character flaw that runs counter to the responsibilities or qualities associated with the hero. What is our hero's character flaw? Bitterness. Here's another problem—this character flaw does not run counter to the qualities and/or responsibilities of his position or situation.

The fact that we're encountering problems is great—we see how useful this formula is as an analytical tool, allowing us to spot the weaknesses in our story.

So, our hero's flaw, bitterness, doesn't run counter to what we expect of a "slacker." Of course the hero's going to be bitter—that's part of his "job description" as a Gen-xer. So the flaw doesn't work.

When I wrote "The Server," I had analyzed more than 5,000 scripts, rewritten scripts for companies as large as the Cannell Studios, and had written half a dozen of my own screenplay. And I still made a fatal, fundamental error! But the important point is that our high concept formula allowed me to finally understand that error. It may be too late for "The Server," because the errors are so fundamental that a rewrite would be as extensive as just writing a whole new script. But, our high concept formula certainly works as an analytical tool.

How would I, as a script doctor, "fix" "The Server?" Well, if someone came to me with a hero who is an apathetic, irreverent Gen-xer, I would put that slacker into the most unlikely position possible to create an instant conflict. I might, for instance, have had him inherit a relative's huge business, and then be forced to try to run it in order to avoid having the business and its employees going under.

A slacker trying to run a fortune 500 company is funny and high concept. A slacker trying to track down a terrorist is not funny or high concept enough to generate excitement. The fact that the hero is a slacker is not necessary to the story. This is a story of *someone* trying to stop a terrorist from blowing up Los Angeles. *Who* that someone is is irrelevant. So we've broken another of the "rules" of high concept: the hero's position or profession isn't related to either the event or the flaw.

Can we fix "The Server?" Yes. But, as I sometimes tell clients, this is a case in which the "fix" would take more energy than would writing a whole new script. But, this too is worth knowing. By using our high-concept formula, we have been able to quickly and accurately determine what was wrong with my script, and been able to ascertain that it's probably more efficient for me to just go on to my next project. That's certainly worth knowing, and frees me from trying vainly to fix "The Server." It also gave me a great idea for that next script: "A Generation X, irresponsible 'slacker' inherits a business that he has to learn how to run.

But let's not cop out. Let's explore "The Server" a little more.

Two approaches

There are two possible approaches to making "The Server" more high concept: we can change either the lifechanging event, or the hero and his flaw.

Given the same hero, a rebellious, anti-establishment, irresponsible slacker, the strongest kind of lifechanging event would be one which would force him to choose between his flawed lifestyle and some opportunity. Let's say he falls in love with a woman who is wealthy and educated and refined, and our hero comes to believe that the only way he can win that woman is to become like her—wealthy, erudite, classy. Now he has to choose between his iconoclasm/rebelliousness/anti-establishmentarianism and the opportunity of being with the woman he's fallen in love with.

This could be a nice romantic comedy, and a fairly high concept little movie that can be clearly stated in a sentence or two: "A rebellious Gen Xer falls in love with a beautiful, upper class woman and decides he must become as refined and successful as she is in order to win her love."

This actually works rather nicely, and easy to state, as any good high-concept piece should be. This could be either a low-budget film like "When Harry Met Sally" or a high budget, star-driven romantic comedy. The problem, is that there is nothing left of the original "Server." That's okay, except that what we're doing isn't *fixing* "The Server," but rather taking one single element from it to write an entirely different script. This is also okay, because if the new script sells, we'll never give a damn about the original "Server" still being flawed.

Now, let's see if we can *keep* the lifechanging event, but change the *hero* to make "The Server" work.

The lifechanging event is our hero being framed for murder. Okay, so what's the problem? The problem is that the lifechanging event itself has been done a million, million times. Hundreds, maybe thousands of movies have been written around a hero being framed for murder.

Killer popes and frumpy housewives

Is there any way of making the hero so unusual that it becomes high concept for them to be framed for murder? Yes. The Pope is framed for murder. The alien ambassador from another planet is framed for murder. A 90-year-woman is framed for murder.

Are these high concepts? Not yet. We have still to connect the three elements of high concept: hero's profession/situation, flaw and lifechanging event. If the pope is framed for murder, how does being framed for murder relate to either his profession or to his flaw? Let's fill in the blanks. The pope, corrupted by the power and prestige of his position, is framed for the murder of a former mistress, by an ambitious Bishop, and must find a way to clear his name without destroying the church.

The ambassador from the first extraterrestrial race to contact Earth, is framed for murder by a right-wing religious leader, and must survive long enough to convince a panicked planet Earth that he is not the vanguard of a murderous alien invasion.

A bitter, self-pitying old woman stuck in a nursing home by her uncaring family, decides to give her fortune to a pet shelter, and is framed for murder by a relative trying to take control of her estate. She must prove her innocence, while fleeing from the police, the tabloid press and her own murderous family.

These log lines are off the top of my head. I'm sure that, by using the high concept formula and other tools in this book, they can be honed to an even higher level. Are they evocative? Certainly. I can see scenes in which the old lady, wheelchair-bound, has to flee the police, escape from jail, using her wits, befriends a young female tabloid journalists who's hounding her for an interview and making her a national cause celebre, a "Grandma Dynamite" kind of folk hero.

I can see the Pope, all pomp and ceremony, forced to suddenly take stock of his life and the questionable decisions he has made as a member of the church hierarchy: his WWII collaboration with the Nazis in order to avoid harm to the Church, perhaps an affair or two, and the fact that the Bishop who wants to kill him has a valid point: the Pope is doing to the Church what Clinton has done for the Presidency: make a mockery of it, threatening to destroy it.

Now this essentially good man who has misplaced his goodness, must find it again so that he can do the right thing, while trying to figure out how he saves the Church from being destroyed by a scandal including his being framed for murder, his past affairs and Nazi affiliation, and the Bishop's own murderous intent. And what if the woman who was killed, whose death he is being blamed for, was the wrong woman—she was a *friend* of his former lover, and as he flees the Bishop's killers, he seeks out the woman who really was his lover so many, many years before.

The formula works!

These are all still rough because they're still dripping ink from the press, but they are also all potentially high concept. The real point here, though, is that the formula works in many dramatically effective ways: it allows us to analyze our stories to see if the concepts are solid; it allows us to create high concepts to build our stories around those concepts; it helps us determine if our concepts are sound enough to be worth pursuing, and; it allows us to see the weaknesses before we commit to writing a script based on those weaknesses.

Fixing the most successful film of all time

Okay, here's one last challenge. Let's fix the most successful film of all time, a film that made more money than any film in history, and won as many Academy Awards as any film in history: "Titanic."

CHAPTER THIRTY

IT'S A WRAP

"This pipsqueak is going to fix *what* film!?"

I can hear you now: "Is he nuts? He wants to fix the most successful script ever written?" Yes, because it desperately needs fixing. In fact, the movie succeeded in *spite* of an extremely weak script, not *because* of it. The Academy of Motion Picture Arts and Science recognized this by giving "Titanic" just about every one of its awards, but withholding even a *nomination* for best screenplay.

How does a film win best picture without even being *nominated* for best screenplay? I'll tell you how: it wins by beating the public into submission with $250 million dollars of special effects, the biggest advertising budget in history, and the biggest opening (most number of theaters) of any film in history.

Using the tools

What do I have to back up my obviously minority opinion? I have the tools in this very book, and watch out, because I'm not afraid to use them. So let's look at the three main elements: the hero and his or her position/profession, the lifechanging event and the hero's flaw.

Who's the hero of "Titanic?" It's actually unclear—it's either DiCaprio's character or Kate Winslett's. This makes it difficult to figure out what the flaw is, but let's say for the sake of argument that the hero is Kate Winslett.

Her flaw? Here we have another problem, because she was loaded down with flaws: spoiled, moody, immature, whiny, rebellious. She's allowed her mother to talk her into marrying a man for money rather than love, so there's some kind of flaw there, I suppose. But from the very beginning Winslett is defying her mother, making it clear she doesn't want to marry the rich guy. She's doing everything she can to sabotage the marriage, so I'm not sure that she really has a flaw except that she doesn't have the maturity or consideration to be honest with her fiancee, but rather sneaks around behind his back, embarrassing him, rather than having the courage to tell him the truth.

This is why the screenplay did not receive critical acclaim, although for some reason the film itself did: several of the major story elements are unclear, including who the hero is, and what the flaw is.

So, we know at least two things that need to be "fixed": hero and flaw. So let's go on to the third major element of high concept: the lifechanging event that forces the hero to choose between her flaw and some opportunity.

There are really only two major events in the film: Winslett falling in love with DiCaprio, and the ship sinking. The sinking of the ship doesn't happen till far too late in the film to be an effective lifechanging event. Also, because it's unclear what her flaw is, it's difficult to know how either the sinking of the ship or falling in love with DiCaprio can force Winslett's character to choose between her flaw and some opportunity. It's also unclear what the opportunity is.

In fact the only thing that seems clear is that nothing is very clear in "Titanic." This is probably what kept the script, DiCaprio and

Winslett from being honored at the Oscars—the script and the roles were not written strongly enough to deserve recognition, even from an Academy apparently desperate to give this film the benefit of the doubt.

However, there *is* an element of high concept to this script. Two lovers fall in love, on the maiden voyage of the "Titanic." It's strong, even though it lacks a second act. So, let's use our formula to create a stronger hero, flaw and act one event.

Let's make Kate Winslett the hero. Her flaw? Let's make it that she's given up on her one, true love in order to marry for money. Let's make it *her* decision and her decision *alone* to marry for money. That way we'll be clear that it's *her* flaw, not her mother's. Instead of her trying to sabotage her engagement to her fiance, she's doing everything she can to convert it into an actual wedding so that she can be the rich lady of the house.

Okay, who's the opponent? It can be the fiancee, I suppose. Or, it could be a story in which the opponent and the hero's ally are the same person, which often happens in love stories, such as "When Harry Met Sally." So let's make DiCaprio's character both the opponent and the hero's ally. He opposes the hero's desire to sell herself to her rich fiance, but DiCaprio is also the hero's ally in that he is the one best suited to helping the hero overcome her flaw, which is greed, born of desperation and poverty.

Now, another problem with "Titanic" is that the romance between the two callow youths happens over far too short a period of time to be believable. So, let's fix that. Let's say that Winslett's character is a tad bit older, perhaps her mid-twenties. She's engaged to a wealthy American. They board the Titanic, the rich fiance intending to bring her home to an American wedding.

As they board the ship, Winslett sees the lower-class passengers being herded aboard like cattle, and she feels upset and guilty. Then she sees him: a man her own age, a tall, ruggedly handsome Irishman. It's the lover she abandoned in order to be with her rich fiancee. He is the lover she truly loves—with her heart, rather than with her purse.

Now the stage is much more nicely set. The passion between Winslett and her lover already exists, so we don't have to worry about the glaring fact that a few days aboard ship isn't enough time to develop a believable romance of any depth.

The conflict already exists, between Winslett's passion and her greed. The other conflict is also already set: Winslett turns out to be not from a family that has fallen on hard times, but from a lower class family like that of her lover's, and she's consciously chosen to abandon her class, and her people. But here comes the lover, representing not only the love she's abandoned, but also the people she's abandoned, the country, the economic and social class she's rejected in favor of wealth gotten under false pretenses.

Now, the Titanic actually has some relevance. You see, in the current Titanic, the ship has nothing to do with anything. The sinking takes place far too late to be an effective act one event. Neither of the main characters really have anything to do with the ship, nor does the hero's flaw. But if the hero's flaw is clearly greed, and it has led her to abandon her own people, and she boards a ship that is the ultimate symbol of 20th century greed in the face of worldwide poverty, then there is a very strong connection between her flaw, the ship and her lover. The ship becomes a symbol.

What is the lifechanging event? The event is discovering that her lover is aboard the ship. Why? Because this event will force her to choose between her greed and the opportunity of being with the man she really loves. And the background is now quite powerful:

she has thrown her lot in with the rich and powerful, and sits on the top decks of the most luxurious ship in the world, while the poor passengers, including her own lover, huddle miserably below decks.

Every minute becomes Winslett's conscious choice to abandon her lover, her people, her class, her heart. Every minute that she sees her lover among the cattle-like lower-class passengers, while she wears beautiful clothes and hobnobs with beautiful people, every such minute becomes an indictment and a challenge to her. Seeing her lover among the disadvantaged and poorly-treated passengers forces her to choose over and over between the luxury symbolized by the Titanic first class, and the opportunity of being below decks with the only man she loves.

Now, with her lover being someone she's already felt deeply for, it's more believable that she would be this much in love, and that she would feel this torn between her lover and the chance of being a millionaire's wife. In James Cameron's film the romance between DiCaprio and Winslett isn't believable because they are too young and have known each other for too short time to believe that it could be a truly deep, dramatic love.

In our new version, when Winslett finally chooses, it's between a deep love and a deep greed, rather than between a life of luxury and life with some uncultured street urchin whose main quality seems to be the ability to spit overboard. In our version, the struggle is also between Winslett's past and future, her people and her own selfish desires, abandoning her culture, her country, her family, and friends and lover.

In James Cameron's "Titanic," Winslett's character seems like an idiot for throwing away a lifetime of wealth for a fling with someone she doesn't even know, someone with absolutely nothing to offer her, financially or emotionally. DiCaprio's character isn't old enough or mature enough to offer her real love. He's essentially an irresponsible, uncultured street urchin, and their life together is bound to be an unhappy, poverty-ridden failure. But with an older lover with whom she *already has* a substantial history and a substantial passionate love, a love that also represents her people, her country, her class and even her own family, she has a tremendous amount to lose by being with the rich guy, and the whole story makes more sense.

So the story becomes one of an ambitious young Irish woman who abandons her one true love, as well as her family, country and heritage, to marry for money, boards a luxury liner with her rich fiance, headed for an American wedding, only to discover her lover's followed her aboard . . . on the maiden voyage of the Titanic.

The log line's too long, but it's already miles better than Cameron's log line: a callow young woman engaged to a wealthy man she does not love, takes up with a young street urchin who teaches her to spit and has sex with her in the back seat of a car, on the maiden voyage of the Titanic.

Look at how disjointed those elements are, how weak the log line is. What's the event? What's her flaw? How do the elements *relate* to each other, *cause* each other, *arise* from each other, *magnify* each other? In James Cameron's version, they don't.

Here's my "Titanic" test: quote me one memorable line from "Titanic." Here is the only response I've ever gotten to that question: "Jack, this is where we first met." I can quote you a dozen great lines from "Casablanca" off the top of my head. "Gone With the Wind," "Forrest Gump," "Steel Magnolias," "Postcards from the Edge," all have great lines associated with them. That's because they were films whose elements meshed, and reinforced each other.

What this book is about

That, in the end, is what this book is about. Would I like to be receiving the writer's residuals from "Titanic?" You betcha, and, if I were James Cameron, I wouldn't care what some schmuck like Rob Tobin said about the quality of the script. But, as Rob Tobin, what I really want is to help *you*, and as many other people as possible, to write screenplays that not only sell, but that make me cry, give me feelings in my gut and down my spine, make me love, make me break down and examine my own life, and make me want to shout in triumph and joy or anger and indignation.

I cried as Forrest stood over his lover's grave, she having finally come home to him, but too late.

I cried when Tom Hanks, in "Big," huddled in a cheap motel room, a little boy having awoken in a man's body.

I cried through half of "Steel Magnolias" and yet somehow felt the victory in Sally Fields affirming that she wouldn't have missed a moment of being a mother to her now dead daughter.

I laughed through "Airplane," "Blazing Saddles," "Young Frankenstein" and "Being There."

And, though I saw the gaping holes in "Saving Private Ryan," I recognized that Spielberg's first half hour of raw, shocking war footage would make that film as important as any ever made.

This is what I want—for brilliant screenplays to be written, screenplays that make a difference to the world, regardless of who writes them. And if this book helps *one* of you to write *one* more "Forrest Gump" or "Cassablanca," then it will have been more than just worthwhile, it will stand as one of my life's main achievements.

Write your hearts out . . . and write your hearts *in*—in to your stories. And follow the formula that has led to the making of the greatest films of all time:
"Casablanca"
"Forrest Gump"
"Steel Magnolias"
"Big"
"Raiders of the Lost Ark"
"Star Wars"
"Back to the Future"
"Close Encounters"
"Saving Private Ryan"
"That Thing You Do"
"The Big Chill"
"Fargo"
"Secrets and Lies"
"Heaven Can Wait"
"Postcards from the Edge"
"Full Monty"
"Princess Bride"
"Airplane"
"Blazing Saddles"

. . . . 'nuff said.

Printed in the United States
105862LV00002B/45/A